GIRLS

GIRLS

Ordinary Girls and Their Extraordinary Pursuits

JENNY McPHEE

LAURA McPHEE

MARTHA McPHEE

RANDOM HOUSE / NEW YORK

Library of Congress Cataloging-in-Publication Data
McPhee, Jenny.
Girls: ordinary girls and their extraordinary pursuits / Jenny McPhee, Laura McPhee,
and Martha McPhee.
p.   cm.
ISBN 0-375-50167-3
1. Girls—United States.   2. Young women—United States.   3. Girls—United States—
Pictorial works.   4. Young women—United States—Pictorial works.   I. McPhee, Laura.
II. McPhee, Martha.   III. Title.
HQ777 .M25 2000   305.23'0973—dc21   00-027574

Book design by J. K. Lambert

For our mother

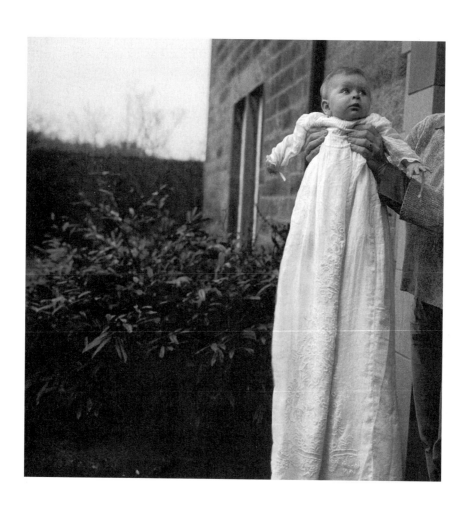

PREFACE

We are a family of girls—five sisters, a strong-minded mother, and an even stronger-minded grandmother, Thelma, who would have you believe that our family was made only of women.

A favorite story of Grammy's was about a time when I, Martha, was three weeks old. I was a bundled newborn in our mother's arms, her fourth daughter, born six years after the first. My three older sisters, Laura, Sarah, and Jenny, swarmed at our grandmother's feet in matching outfits our mother had sewn out of fabric from Liberty. We were on the lawn at my grandmother's house in Maine beneath an American flag fluttering in the stiff sea breeze. It was 1964. The Atlantic Ocean spread vast in front of us, and the air smelled of salt and pine. "Here," my mother is reported to have said, handing me to her mother. "You can have this one. I've already got three."

"That's simply not true," our mother would say about the story her mother told.

No matter the truth, I was one more girl for Grammy's clan, one more girl to march intrepidly over time in a line of female ancestors that reached back two, three hundred years. My sisters and I followed in the path of Maid Marian of Scotland, who loved to ride horses and had a keen passion for medicine; of Nancy Cooper, cousin of the great James Fenimore and the first woman in our family to earn a higher degree—which she did during the Civil War at Richmond Seminary; of Glenna, an itinerant schoolteacher in the Wild West; of Thelma, our grandmother, a registered nurse at the Brooklyn Hospital; of Pryde, our mother, an accomplished portrait photographer and the grandmother of two girls, so far anyway, and one surprise boy.

When our grandmother was in the hospital dying of heart failure, Laura was seven months pregnant with the baby who would become Isobel Justine. On a chalkboard in her room Laura wrote Isobel's name so that Grammy could see it from her bed. Isobel was still just a little octopus in her mother's womb, kicking and turning and bouncing with life as our grandmother was quietly dying. "No, no," Grammy declared emphatically, seeing the name. "That cannot be her name. You must name her Glenna. Name her Glenna for my mother. Glenna was a strong woman. Glenna is a strong name." Her determined, sharp green eyes held Laura. Isobel was of her, of Thelma, and would be hers, a baby bundle in a blanket in her arms on a lawn in Maine. Possessively Grammy pressed her hand to Laura's belly. She was placing Isobel in her matriarchy, giving her a role, dreaming Isobel's future so that she could glimpse it.

Not long after our grandmother's death, Jenny became pregnant with a son. A son? None of us knew what we would do with a boy! Indeed, Jenny cried upon learning this news. He was the first boy in our family in a long time. Jenny named him Tommaso after our grandmother Thelma, whose nickname was Tommy. Now, at three, surrounded by his aunts and his best friend, Isobel, he often asks if he can wear dresses when he becomes a girl, if he can grow his hair long, wear high heels and lipstick when he becomes a girl. At the same time he and Isobel run around the house dressed in cowboy costumes, wielding swords, and shooting pistols.

We began work on this book in the fall of 1997. The idea of having a baby girl myself was still a distant fantasy, though my desire to have a daughter fueled my curiosity about the state of girlhood in this country. As we finished the book two years later I learned that I was pregnant and that the baby was a girl. I could see my grandmother holding her, imagine her looking at the baby and sighing and exclaiming, as she loved to do when something thrilled her—"I've died and gone to heaven." In the sonogram picture, the baby was a big-eyed thing with a vast forehead and an anxious little frown peering out of the chthonic depths. She seemed to be expressing concerned curiosity about what was outside, in the same way, it seemed, as we were wondering, speculating, anticipating what was inside—who will Livia be?

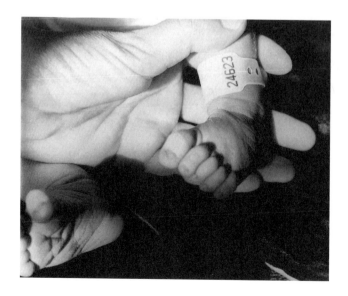

INTRODUCTION

We drove across America to talk with girls—girls from a variety of landscapes and communities and backgrounds, ordinary girls pursuing passions and dreams. We traveled through the rolling golden hills of the Palouse of eastern Washington, along the shaded banks of the San Antonio River, onto the trading floor of a brokerage firm in the dizzying heights of a Dallas skyscraper. We spoke with a girl who competes in the dying sport of sidesaddle riding; a Hmong girl who became an American citizen. We talked with a blues-rock musician, ballerinas, surfers, an ice skater, a girl who plays with dolls.

Driving across Arizona from east to west, we passed through the center of a Navajo reservation. Against a slate-blue sky, rain and lightning descended from luminous thunderheads. The ravines and plateaus at the edge of the Painted Desert shifted from rose to yellow. We watched the rain approach and pass; lightning touched ground with astounding frequency. We were overwhelmed by nature's display, by the sparsity of the population, by the difference between this impressive landscape and the mild places we come from.

In the small desert town of Ganado on the reservation, we met Alvina Begay, a Navajo. Alvina is eighteen and runs track competitively. She has also run toward the rising sun as a rite of passage. Her hair, uncut since birth, is a Navajo symbol of knowledge. "The rain you see in the distance, streaming down from the clouds, the rain is the hair, and the cloud is the Navajo knot," she explained. "It represents my knowledge and my fertility. Water feeds the land."

The day before, in Phoenix, we had interviewed Jennifer Williams, a young woman from rural Texas whose parents' ambition for her was an early marriage and kids. Instead, she is engaged in brain-tumor research and is on her way to college and medical school. We also met Kory Johnson, who founded Children for a Safe Environment as a response to the death of her sister from congenital heart disease caused by hazardous waste. On the south rim of the Grand Canyon, we interviewed four very young Girl Scouts who go camping in the canyon.

For us, the experience of meeting each girl in this book was inspiring and unexpected. We knew them to be ordinary girls with passion, girls like many others we know who have embraced their chosen pursuits as a center of meaning in their lives. Most often girls told us they feel pleasure at being good at something, at having the discipline and perseverance to see that they could improve, even excel, at a given endeavor. But no matter how extraordinary their accomplishments, all the girls saw themselves as fundamentally ordinary. We were often deeply moved by the obstacles girls had to overcome, by the circumstances from which they had blossomed with wonderful confidence and humility. Meeting these girls was an opportunity for us to see the diversity of girlhood in America today, to sense where girls are going, to understand influences brought to bear from the past, and to gain a glimpse of the future for the half of the population that is female.

To a person, the girls we met had ambitions and believed that there were no limits on the possibilities they envisioned for their futures. Glass ceilings and other sorts of discrimination seemed not to enter their thoughts. They

talked of becoming pediatricians, FBI agents, astronauts, teachers, lawyers, brain surgeons, painters, poets, playwrights. They also believed that these pursuits were entirely consistent with motherhood and family life. While their assumptions sometimes seemed naïve to us, they were also encouraging. It impressed us that they saw the world as fully open to them, that the women's movement and the quest for equal rights had succeeded so completely when it came to influencing the beliefs of young women. Many of them knew that the situation was "easier" or "better" for them than it had been for their mothers and grandmothers. Some knew that a woman's right to vote was only comparatively recently won. Quite a few were familiar with Title IX (a clause in the 1972 Education Act stating that no one shall because of sex be denied the benefits of any educational program or activity that receives direct federal aid) and had opinions about its effectiveness. But for most of them the word *feminism* (if it was understood as distinct from *feminine*) was a slur or an epithet— certainly a label to be avoided. By and large, the history of the feminist movement and its political achievements were not clearly understood.

With one exception, the girls we talked with embraced being female. They were proud of their belief that they have every opportunity boys have, and then some. They talked about the fact that they could openly enjoy clothes and dressing up and shopping and the realm of the emotional. Whenever we asked the question "Do you like being a girl?" we were struck by the vehemence of the affirmative response.

———

For many years now we three have spoken of girls, and of collaboration, and when we arrived at the idea of doing a book together about girls and girlhood in America we felt elated. We started collaborating when we were children. Laura, the oldest, would organize us into a theater troupe. In the basement playroom we put on elaborate productions of stories that we invented to-gether—stories, of course, that always had to do with girls, strong and resilient girls, girls who did things, who had adventures that took them around the world. Through play we became curious about the process of transforming re-alities, turning the real into the imagined and going places with it. Later we wrote stories and poems, learned photography and gymnastics. These en-deavors gave us confidence as children. People—our parents, our friends, our grandparents, aunts, and teachers—were our audience. Their attention, en-couragement, and enthusiasm made us proud of what we were doing.

Our experiences, however, date from the sixties and seventies, the heyday of the women's movement. Our mother, a photographer, belonged to the Na-tional Organization for Women almost from its inception and also to a group called Women on Words and Images. That group authored two seminal stud-ies on how children's readers used in public schools overwhelmingly depicted girls and women as unambitious, unathletic, passive, and even foolish. From a young age, we were made explicitly aware of the ways in which words and im-ages influence culture. Now, as mothers ourselves, we are drawn anew to the subject of girlhood, wishing to understand how the experience of being a girl has altered in the intervening years and trying to discover what makes things right for girls, what makes them feel affirmed in their power and leads them to experience life in a full and complex manner.

In this book, we wanted to look at ordinary girls and make a record both vi-sual and verbal of the extraordinary things that girls do and of the drives and desires that lead them to do those things. The world has broadened for girls, but we also saw that girls still struggle with discrimination in sports despite Title IX; they are still beset with bulimia and anorexia, which predominantly strike teenage girls; they still suffer crises of self-esteem beginning in the third grade

and earlier despite influential work calling attention to this issue; and they often have difficulty negotiating body image and self-image in a world that relentlessly promotes stick figures for women, consumer fashion, and the cult of celebrity. For *Girls,* we have sought out real-world girls in order to explore their attitudes and lives, their creative acts, perseverance, and discipline, their successes, joys, and disappointments. We hope that these girls may speak for others and be role models, not only through the range of their interests but also through their forthrightness, their openness, and their desire to share.

Eleanor Roosevelt once remarked that one of the proudest moments in her life was when she made the first team in field hockey. She acknowledged the deep roles of teamwork and competition in developing her ability to be the great leader and achiever that she was. Dr. Sylvia Rimm, in *See Jane Win,* notes that the "most positive experience remembered by successful women was winning in competition." She also states that the parents of successful women had high expectations for them (regardless of their own level of success or education) and that membership in a girl group such as the Girl Scouts was of tremendous importance in building self-esteem. Meanwhile, lack of self-esteem—usually associated with issues of beauty and popularity—is still the number-one problem for girls. In recent years numerous groundbreaking works have studied the social problems of American girls with depth and intelligence, including extraordinary books such as Carol Gilligan's *Meeting at the Crossroads* and *In a Different Voice* and Mary Pipher's *Reviving Ophelia.* *Girls* acknowledges the problems girls face, but its primary focus is on the myriad ways in which girls have taken hold of their worlds and shaped them to affirm their sense of self. We hope that this book will offer a view of girlhood that resonates with the wonderful things that girls have created and achieved, in collaboration with their parents, coaches, teachers, mentors, and friends.

The first girl we talked with was Kara-Lee Alexander. We heard about her while we were eating dinner in a lobster shack in Maine. We struck up a conversation with our waitress, and she told us about a sixteen-year-old friend who spent her spare hours fishing for lobster and tuna at ledges far out to sea. Word of mouth was a significant resource for us, as were newspapers and the Internet. Acquaintances told us about twins who skied, a very young champion chess player, a girl with an abiding interest in meteorology, a painter with a style like Picasso's. Girls we interviewed told us about other girls. We crisscrossed the country finding, interviewing, and photographing girls and being amazed at the range of choices they've made, and at the wisdom, discipline, and compassion they possess. We know that this book is just a beginning, that these girls have fascinating, accomplished sisters everywhere—and that there is something of the girls we met in every girl.

Pryde Brown

IMAGINATION

Imagination—in their lives, their choices—united all the girls we talked with, whether they are in this book or part of the chorus behind it.

"Imagination Jersey City Hall" is something our grandmother Thelma used to say. She repeated it frequently, moving her hand in a circular motion at her ear to indicate a sort of crazy fondness for the world that we implicitly understood. "Imagination Jersey City Hall" meant nothing logical, but as it is perfect iambic pentameter, it sounded wonderful to the ear. Privately, we would try to interpret the phrase. Grammy was married at Jersey City Hall, and perhaps the phrase held all the dreams she had about what marriage meant and where her future would lead her. Often she would tell us that if a situation had not unfolded as she would have liked, she would simply rewrite it by telling the history as it should have been. Through storytelling she developed her imagination, one that she did her level best to impart to us with her elaborate tales about our family's origins.

She was a cowgirl in Montana. Her mother, the itinerant schoolteacher, left Grammy and her younger sister alone for months on end. At night our grandmother and her sister would curl in bed together, as she would do with us some fifty years later, and tell tales of how they were descended from Scottish aristocracy and the German intellectual elite. She came from princesses and queens and fearless women in America who earned incomes long before that was common for a woman. There was a milliner for William Howard Taft's grandmother; an entrepreneur who started pineapple-canning empires and breweries; a clergywoman at Richmond Seminary during the Civil War; a world-class harpist; a Shakespearean scholar; and somehow, Thelma's great-grandmother had passed on to her General George Armstrong Custer's shaving kit. The list of female accomplishment was endless. *Imagination Jersey City Hall*—the phrase stood for the possibility of storytelling, and her stories were about writing a place for herself, a personal history, so she could stand tall, expressed and understood, against the infinite universe.

In our travels across the country for this book, we saw in the girls we met different stages and expressions of imagination. In New York City we spent Halloween afternoon with a group of very young girls and found that their choices of costume reflected their fantasies, stimulated, of course, by what they had discovered in our culture. We passed time with little girls playing dress-up—the trunk hauled out of the closet, spilling tutus and tiaras and sparkling Dorothy shoes and sequined gowns and lots of lace and ruffles, taffeta and organza. All the fabrics and colors, a collage of dreams. The girls would slip in and out of outfits as if trying on the possibilities of who they would become as grown women, or at least of what articulated best who they thought themselves to be at that moment. Watching them was a way to see ideas they had about themselves for which they did not yet have a vocabulary.

The majority of girls we spoke with said that one of the things that they loved best about being female was dressing up and looking beautiful, putting on a little makeup, buying something special and feeling magnificent in it. Many noted that they felt sorry that boys are not allowed this privilege and grateful that it is theirs. Whether it was the brain-tumor researcher or the ballerinas we were speaking with, they saw their beauty and style as something to celebrate, a powerful part of their self-definition.

If our grandmother had lived in a different time, she would have been an artist—a painter or a writer, for she enjoyed both. Her mother, Glenna, was a musician who played the harp and the piano, had the high soprano of an opera singer, and could recite almost any part from Shakespeare. Though her family was close to impoverished, Glenna dressed well and had a trunk full of fine clothes—linens and lace and silks—that accompanied her as they moved from place to place across the West. When Glenna was away teaching, her daughters would empty her trunk to invoke her presence. Dressed in her velvets, they performed plays they created themselves. Wearing her clothes made them feel more grown up, more inventive, not so much alone.

At the bottom of this magical trunk was a china doll named Pearl Honey Dew. When they were bored with dressing up, they played with Pearl. They pretended she was their baby, and they taught her to sing and recite Shakespeare and promised her they would never leave. Throughout our childhood we played with Pearl when we visited our grandmother. When eventually Pearl broke, my grandmother had a burial for her beneath the pines in her backyard, telling us that Pearl had lived many dreams.

In Flemington, New Jersey, Patricia Raubo showed us her collection of dolls and explained to us her "doll theory." For a seventh-grader, playing with dolls is no longer "cool," so she plays with them in secret now. Her dolls are an important part of her world, and she refuses to let them go. She believes that playing with dolls has taught her to be generous and nurturing, and that boys should be encouraged to play with them as well. She feels it would make life easier all around. Recent studies confirm Patricia's point that playing with dolls teaches empathy. And it is also a way to dream and enact fantasy and give voice to the interior life.

With some of the girls we interviewed, imagination had been transformed into art—poetry, paintings, novels, videos, musical compositions. Chloe

Cheimets started writing sonnets spontaneously when she was seven years old after seeing a total eclipse of the sun. She explained to us that she wanted to give words to her vision of the natural world as a way of understanding the awe she felt. As a two-year-old, Alexandra Nechita started painting and has not stopped at thirteen. She feels driven by a power that is beyond her, but the canvases represent every part of her—all the confusion and beauty that is inside. Mina Blyly-Strauss escapes to the world seen from behind the lens of her video camera, trying to create an order that will help her understand the pain of her little brother's close call with death. The art these girls have made, of course, is a more sophisticated expression of the interior life than is a game of dress-up or dolls, but the essence is the same: to escape, to imagine, to dream, to interpret, to understand, to explore, to give, to voice, to speak.

ON HALLOWEEN

—

New York City

EVELYN SAYLOR

———

Composer and pianist

Evelyn Saylor has thick chestnut hair and a demure manner. Her fingers are long and slender, agile. She has been playing the piano and composing short pieces since she was four. When Evelyn was six she was one of a handful of children selected to play at the Bard Music Festival at Bard College. She played Tchaikovsky's "The Sick Doll" and "The New Doll." That same year she was asked to play at New York City's Symphony Space in the Wall to Wall Bach program. She was one of the first students to attend the Special Music School of America in New York City, a new public school for musically gifted children. *Good Morning America* profiled the school when it first opened, and Evelyn was selected to play on that segment.

We visit the Saylors one brisk Sunday morning in March. Two teenage girls greet us at the door of a brownstone on New York City's Upper West Side. One of them holds a baby on her hip. "Are you the women who want to talk to Evelyn?" they ask, suspicion, protectiveness, and pride all hovering in the cadences of their voices. We are led into a cozy living room where an upright piano fits snugly in one corner. Framed concert programs and posters cover the walls.

The girls' parents, Constance Beavon (a mezzo-soprano) and Bruce Saylor (a composer who has worked closely with soprano Jessye Norman), introduce us to their four daughters. For the next few hours we sit in the sun-flooded room, drinking tea and discussing art, writing, sisters, family history. We speak of New York, and above all, of music.

"We all have music swimming around our heads," Bruce explains. "The girls have had perfect pitch from a very young age."

"It's really in the blood," Constance adds. "My grandmother had three sisters, and they all sang, and my mother and her sister and a friend sang in a trio."

Since she was two, Evelyn, now seven, has been taking classes in Dalcroze Eurythmics. Swiss musician Émile Jaques-Dalcroze believed that rhythm is the primary element of music and developed an approach to music education based on rhythmic movement and the use of the whole body. In Dalcroze classes children learn and explore musical concepts such as meter, tempo, phrase, form, and dynamics through rhythm games, creative movement, songs, stories, ear training, solfège, and improvisation. Young instrumentalists with Dalcroze training typically progress quickly because they understand the elements of music and because their bodies have already been trained in rhythmic expression. They also find practice less tedious and performance more natural.

Although Evelyn loves to play Tchaikovsky, Bach, and Beethoven, her true love is composing. "I love to fiddle around on the piano and make little pieces.

Then I put them together, then I change them. The hard part is getting them in the order I want. But when I'm done I love to play my pieces for Mommy and Daddy and my sisters and Irina, my piano teacher."

For us she plays "Frère Jacques," then plays it backward.

"Play something of yours," one of her sisters urges.

"How about 'The Invention'?" another sister suggests. "Or 'Happy and Sad'?"

"No, no. Play 'The Time Machine.' It is such a good story."

Evelyn plays a short complicated piece that jumps from soothing to scary to playful to joyous.

"I made up this song about a tall, skinny inventor guy," Evelyn explains, "and he invents a time machine and then travels back in time. When he gets out of the machine, he doesn't know where he is but it's this really beautiful place and then he sees a brontosaurus and he knows he's in dinosaur times. Then there's a thunderstorm and he sees a big tyrannosaurus rex and he gets really scared so he gets back in the time machine and goes back home and he is so happy to go home."

ALEXANDRA NECHITA

—

Painter

Walking into Alexandra Nechita's studio at her sprawling neoclassical home near Los Angeles is like walking into a collage. Alexandra is only thirteen years old, yet the walls are covered from floor to ceiling with newspaper and magazine clippings about her from all over the world: *Time, Newsweek, Le Monde, L'Espresso, Der Spiegel,* to name only a few. The headlines read, "Prodigy," "Genius," "A Young Picasso," "Picasso Incarnate." Against one wall are her paintings and canvases, stacked several deep. Spread about the floor are her paints and brushes. She's been in *Vogue,* on *The Oprah Winfrey Show.* Galleries in New York, Paris, and Los Angeles represent her work. She tours the world regularly for exhibitions. Her paintings sell for as much as $200,000. Her large house with many rooms and a pool is the result of the success of Alexandra's art. Contributing to her family in this way is, she says, her honor. Her family is the most important thing to her.

Alexandra epitomizes the American dream of success. She was born in Communist Romania in 1986. Her father fled the country for America, leaving behind Alexandra's mother, who was six months pregnant. When Alexandra was a year and a half, she and her mother followed. At two she was painting. At eight she had her first exhibit in a local library (where she sold her first painting, for fifty dollars). At nine, after another exhibit, she signed with an art management company, and by the time she was ten she and her art work were skyrocketing to fame. One might expect her to be the youngest person in attendance at her openings, yet she rarely is because so many families bring their children to meet Alexandra. To hordes of reporters she has explained that she is still in many ways an ordinary child who goes to school and does homework and likes basketball and movies and has girlfriends. The only difference in her curriculum is that she's not required to take art class at school. She studies art in Paris and the South of France, where the previous summer she created her first lithographs, etchings, and ceramics. Ordinary kid that she is, Oprah Winfrey, Whoopi Goldberg, and Andre Agassi are some of the many who own a Nechita painting. Her work hangs in a dozen museums around the world, and an international tour is on the horizon. She has high ambitions. She wants her art to hang in every important museum in the world. "I've got time," she says. "I'm still young."

Her paintings are often described as reminiscent of Picasso and Braque, though Alexandra is not aware of having seen their work before she began painting in this style. When she was eight and having her first show, her mother took her to a Picasso exhibit in Los Angeles. Alexandra was stunned by the similarities and exclaimed to her mother, "He paints just like I do!" Since her schoolmates thought her style wacky and made fun of it, it never occurred to her that others painted as she did. She doesn't mind that people consider her a young Picasso or a young painter or a young anything for that matter. "When I was very small my dream was to be ten years old and a great painter that the world respected. I never wanted to grow older than ten. I wanted to stay ten forever. I'm not sure why I chose ten, but it seemed perfect. I achieved the dream with my art by ten. And the other dream, the dream of staying ten, well, of course that's impossible. But I know I can always feel young. When I'm eighty, if I live that long, I hope the critics still call me 'the young artist.' "

JENN CROWELL

——

Novelist

Jenn Crowell, who grew up in rural Pennsylvania, always wanted to be a writer. Before she knew how to write, she told her family stories and her grandmother wrote them down for her. From an early age she went to any writing workshop or conference that would have her. In seventh grade she wrote a hundred-page sci-fi fantasy. And when she was fourteen she was accepted into the Pennsylvania Governor's School for the Arts summer program for high school artists. There she began a novel.

Determined to flee an overcrowded high school and pursue writing, she graduated at the end of her junior year and went to Goucher College. The novelist Madison Smartt Bell became her mentor. When she told him that she'd written a novel about a thirty-year-old American woman whose English husband dies of leukemia, leaving her alone to bring up their young son, he read it, loved it, and sent it to his agent. In less than two months she had an offer from G. P. Putnam's Sons. In 1997 *Necessary Madness* was published internationally. Jenn was seventeen years old.

"Insightful," "mature," "rich beyond her years" were comments critics used frequently to describe Jenn's writing.

"I was always attracted to older voices in my fiction," she explains. "Had I written about a seventeen-year-old in small-town America, it would have been horrible. In the thick of adolescence, I would have had no perspective on it."

The most difficult thing she had to grapple with upon publication and in the ensuing rush of publicity was how manipulated she felt by the press. "They took every opportunity to portray me as a very young girl and often insisted on photographing me in these childlike poses." As a self-described feminist she was irritated by that—she felt she was being used by the persona-driven publishing industry to tap into the latest trend embracing anything that portrays the sexualized girl-child as powerful. "For example," she clarifies, "the Spice Girls or Fiona Apple. There is not a nuanced perception of girls in our culture," she says. On the other hand, she realized that she would do anything to sell her book. "It was my baby, and I wanted to get it out there, get it read."

Academic work in women's studies has led Jenn to the conclusion that there are many misconceptions about what it means to be a girl in the United States. "I feel ambivalent about the rush of pop psychology books on young women's development," she says. "Part of me thinks it's great that the subject is being addressed, and part of me fears it's only a trend."

She believes a major problem for feminism has been the real lack of dialogue between second-wave feminists and young women. "The younger feminists place a huge emphasis on personal experience and see things like body piercing and tattoos and pornography as empowering. The older feminists find the moral relativism of that position scary, and communication breaks down." But even more disturbing, according to Jenn, is the fact that women uniting to fight for something is still too terrifying a concept for the larger society. "Why is the idea of women banding together still so scary for both women and men?"

CHLOE CHEIMETS

—

Poet

THE LOVELY PLACE

A Sonnet

(written at age seven)

The glittering stars pleasant shine
And flowers steady glow
Both of these sprout on time's long vine
And sway from life's crisp blow
The fairies tap and twirl
The green leaves grow with life
The rainbow's colors blend and swirl
A world with no pain or strife
The sweet raindrops spin across the landscape
Happiness shines down upon this place
This beauty sparks out of the fluffy blue cape
The snow coats the ground like ruffly lace

MINA BLYLY-STRAUSS

—

Video artist

Mina has blue hair. Actually, it's black with a deep tint of blue. The blue shimmers in the sunlight as she sits on a swinging bench in her small front yard on a street in Minneapolis. She is a sixteen-year-old orthodox Jew and wears clothes that reflect her religious beliefs—a below-the-knee skirt and a long-sleeved shirt. She refers to herself as an "extremely active video artist" and tells us that being orthodox has nothing to do with her art—or her blue hair. In the past year she's made three videos: a documentary on the environment and endangered species; one about her baby brother who was born dead and then revived; and one on geometry. She is at work on a video about street theater and a video self-portrait.

In her living room Mina shows us her videos. Something pungent is cooking in the kitchen. Dogs hiding under the couch and chairs bark to protest the continued presence of strangers. Fish swim lazily in a bubbling tank. Baby paraphernalia is strewn about the floor.

Of the videos Mina has made, the most compelling is about her half brother, who was born with a hole in his lung and was not breathing. Surgery revived him, and after weeks in the neonatal intensive care unit he was able to survive on his own. The video captures, in a collage of pictures and interviews and voice-overs, the traumatic effect on the family. It ends happily with the baby on a clear path to recovery—smiling cheekily with outsized sunglasses toppling off his nose.

Mina is shy and quiet but forthcoming. After we watch the video she tells us that the birth of her brother was the hardest thing she has had to deal with. "Before the difficulties of his birth," she says, "before he was born dead, I had always thought I knew what to expect from life, what was coming next. Once he was revived and in the neonatal intensive care unit, none of us knew what would happen next. We had to deal with that. Trust. My artwork has helped me accept that, the unknown. It's scary still, but manageable."

PERFORMERS

Sarah was the performer in our family. She was the ballerina, the pianist, the actress and singer. At Christmas parties she led the guests in carols, standing by the piano, her high soprano rising above the well-lit tree and hanging there softly in the quiet room just long enough to ignite all the other voices. She'd wear a blue velvet gown, her curly hair back in a bandeau, and she'd hold everyone—fifty, sixty people—with her green eyes until they were eager to sing with her. She starred in *The Nutcracker, Kiss Me Kate, Showboat, The Importance of Being Earnest, Swan Lake.* She was Ophelia, Juliet, Desdemona, and Cordelia. "Tragedy is in my veins," she'd say, waltzing through the house in her tutu, on pointe.

Our house was a ranch on a hill in New Jersey. It had been a hunter's cabin but over the years was transformed by additions that radiated spokelike from the original single room. There were lofts and an indoor swimming pool. It was large but falling apart, home to ten kids (our mother had remarried a man with five children) and often many of our friends. Ivy climbed the walls, eating away at the log cabin siding.

The front deck, which our stepfather had designed, was tiered, and it was his intention to use it as a stage from which he would direct productions of Shakespeare featuring all the kids, with Sarah as the lead. But Sarah was the only interested party, and she didn't need direction at home. Alone she practiced her singing, her lines, her positions. She performed with her whole being, turning her body into an instrument of engagement.

———

The image of Sarah in her classical poses trying to differentiate herself from all the other kids in an unwieldy household is reminiscent of some of the girls we met during our travels. We talked to ballerinas in the parking lot of a south L.A. strip mall, to a rapper on the streets of St. Paul, to a beauty queen standing among statues of Roman figures at Caesars Palace on Las Vegas Boulevard. We met a group of young actresses from the Urban Youth Theater in Manhattan; a harpist in Austin, Texas, who played next to an outdoor mural depicting galloping cowboys; and vocalists from the Girls Choir of Harlem in a city playground. The girls distinguish themselves with their bodies and gestures— dramatic representations of their dreams.

For all of these girls, their pursuits are their passions and their way of expressing themselves. Dedication to their form has led them to dance at Joffrey and American Ballet Theater camps, to star in Hollywood films, to win a Grammy for playing the harp, to be a blues-rock musician at thirteen with a thriving fan club and a professional touring outfit.

Often their commitment to their art has helped them get beyond a particular difficulty in their lives—divorce, sickness, eating disorders, poverty—using their hardship as a source of strength, as a resource to build a life rather than as a reason to cave in. Through rapping, Tiffany Jones, a high school dropout, got herself into an arts school that allowed her an education and time to practice and master her "flow." Through acting, Jena Malone changed her life and her mother's. Now instead of living in a car, she stars in movies and they live in a Tudor house outside New York City. Community-supported programs like

the Urban Youth Theater, founded in 1995, have helped cultivate the talents of inner-city teenagers in acting, directing, choreographing, playwriting, design, and technical theater, providing them with an opportunity that might not otherwise have been available to them.

Beauty pageants too are an aspect of performance in America. One hundred thousand girls participate in them annually, mainly in the South. Usually it is at their mothers' instigation, and often the aim is to get the girls out of the small, underprivileged worlds that envelop them. They believe that by winning the cash and scholarship prizes attached to the competitions, their daughters have a chance. In "Beautiful Girls," an essay on child pageants, Susan Orlean writes, "The world of pageants is a system with an organizing principle and a clear set of dreams: the dream that the child will somehow, miraculously, be lifted above and out of her current lot in life. Like winning the lottery or striking gold, or like basketball for the kid in the ghetto, beauty pageants are a version of the American dream, using what the parents and the child understand best: beauty."

The mother of a six-year-old pageant princess we met had ambitions for her daughter: "For us these pageants are the most direct route we know for getting her into college. And I'll do anything for this child to get there."

———

Women have participated publicly in the performing arts for a relatively short time. Before the 1800s, female roles in theater, music, ballet, and so forth were performed primarily by men. During the romantic period in the early nineteenth century, women ballet dancers flourished in France and Russia and later in the United States. The rise of the ballerina opened the door for women in all genres of the performing arts, though progress has been slow. In fact, Lilith Fair—the all-female music festival—was launched in 1997 by singer/songwriter Sarah McLachlan after she was told that more than one woman on a concert bill was bad business. The fair shocked the music industry by grossing more than 44 million dollars in its first two years.

Though the girls we spoke with may or may not continue to pursue their careers as performers, all of them find the experience dynamic and a great source of self-confidence. "To be the object of an entire audience's pleasure is a powerful sensation," said Yasmeen Santos of the Urban Youth Theater.

"Dancing drives me," said Catalina Maese, one of the ballerinas. "It's what motivates me most in life, and I love saying to people that I'm a dancer. I'm addicted. Dancing expresses who I am, and I love to flirt with the audience, have them as mine."

Patricia Marte, also of the Urban Youth Theater, wants to form a production company when she's older, "start small and end up like Miramax." Other girls have more conventional ambitions, to become doctors and lawyers, but acknowledge that whatever happens to them, being onstage now has taught them to stand in front of the world.

KEISHA ACCO, SHENIQUIA GALE,
TIFFANY JONES, AND JETAIME McFADDEN

—

Girls Choir of Harlem

Lorna Myers, director and conductor of the Girls Choir of Harlem, wants her choir to be the best in the world. Not the best girls' choir or children's choir but the best choir. Only one in four choirs in the country are exclusively female, which makes her effort all the more arduous. Traditionally, women and girls were not allowed to sing onstage; their parts were sung by boys. It's only in the last century that this model changed. In 1979 Walter J. Turnbull, founder and conductor of the Boys Choir of Harlem, established the Girls Choir, but not until the past decade has it emerged from the shadow of its famous counterpart. Today in grades four through twelve at the Choir Academy of Harlem, a public school also founded by Mr. Turnbull, there are about 500 girls, with 104 singing in the choir.

A graduate of Juilliard and an accomplished vocalist, Miss Myers sees it as her duty to help effect this change. She's been working with these girls just a few years, and already they've made enormous leaps forward. Miss Myers, a large, imposing, elegant woman with long black hair pulled into a tight bun and an emphatic lilting Trinidadian accent, is tough. She believes in discipline and begins with what might seem to be the small details—poise, dress, walk, manners, diction. She does not tolerate the use of Ebonics, mismatched uniforms, low grades, or poor conduct on the streets, in school, or anywhere else. "A lot of my girls have discipline problems. Their lives at home aren't always easy. But discipline teaches them respect—respect for themselves. I like my girls to have grace." Mostly she teaches them to appreciate music and to learn the range and possibility of their voices. She teaches them classical music in Latin, German, and Italian, using language to take them places they never thought they could go.

"I used to sing in my church choir," says Tiffany Jones when we speak with four high-school-age girls from the school one afternoon. The choir is practicing, and we can hear their voices drifting down the hall. "I thought I could only sing soul and R&B, but here I learned that my voice can stretch to accomplish many more things."

"I feel special," Sheniquia Gale tells us, "because I know these languages. I know what the words mean when I sing these songs. Not everybody can sing all these songs in classical German and hear them and know the meaning."

"To be here you need to be committed," says Keisha Acco. "Most of our time is devoted to the school, to singing, and if we aren't singing we're doing homework because you've got to keep your grades up to be in the choir. I didn't know I had such drive, but knowing that I do makes me feel I can do anything. I want to be a pediatrician."

Miss Myers has them practice several hours every day and throughout the summer. The girls feel Miss Myers is strict, but they respect her and want to work hard for her. In November 1997, a big color picture of the choir appeared on the front page of *The New York Times,* announcing the choir's debut at Lincoln Center's Alice Tully Hall. Requests for other appearances poured in. They sang at Alice Tully again for Christmas 1998. Someday soon the vocalists hope to be touring the world.

"When you're up there on the stage singing for a large audience of family and friends and strangers and famous people," says Jetaime McFadden, "you understand your gift."

JENA MALONE

—

Actor

Before Jena turned ten, she and her mother, Debbie, had been homeless once, on welfare six times, and had even lived in their car. Her father, whom Debbie refers to as "a used-car salesman," left them two weeks after Jena was born. But when they moved to Las Vegas from Lake Tahoe their luck changed. In a newspaper Jena saw an ad seeking "fresh faces." It promised big careers for child stars in films and commercials in exchange for participating in a workshop. Jena scraped together the thousand-dollar fee from money she'd saved selling homemade lemonade and hand-strung bead necklaces and from other odd jobs.

The leader of the workshop was a fraud, but the experience led Jena to an agent, and the agent led Jena to two auditions in Los Angeles. One was for a student film and the other was for a Michael Jackson video entitled "Childhood." Jena got both parts. With two hundred dollars in their pockets, they moved to a tiny, pest-infested apartment in L.A., and within six months Jena was cast as Bone in the made-for-television movie of Dorothy Allison's novel *Bastard Out of Carolina* directed by Anjelica Huston. Soon after, she was cast as the young version of Jodie Foster's character in the feature film *Contact*, then as Ellen in a TV movie based on the book *Ellen Foster* by Kaye Gibbons. She's been working ever since.

—

We meet Jena and Debbie at their home in a town not far from Manhattan. They have recently moved from Los Angeles so that Jena could attend the School for Professional Children in New York City. She is aiming for Oxford University in England, where she intends to study English literature as well as business. But for now, at thirteen, she's making movies and TV shows. In late 1998 she starred in *Stepmom*. She's signed on for a double episode of *Homicide*, a small part in a Kevin Costner film, and a historical film set in Scotland.

Jena is curled into an overstuffed chair in her living room as she listens to her mother tell us her own life story. Debbie, who is thirty-six, has a round, bright face and a strong laugh. She speaks about her daughter with devotion and perhaps a little envy, but also with a sense of awe at what she has created. Debbie's new baby girl, Madison May Malone (Jena named her), crawls across the floor gurgling. Once again Debbie is a single mother. Two weeks after breaking off her engagement to Madison's father she realized she was pregnant. "I was crying and vomiting, but Jena was walking on air—delighted, running around the house saying, 'We're going to have a baby . . .' "

As with the painter Alexandra Nechita, Jena has the very unusual role in her family of being the major breadwinner and thus carries the responsibilities of both the provider and the child. Debbie asks Jena's approval for all major financial decisions, whether it's about renting an expensive house, buying a car, or hiring baby care for Madison.

"We've had difficulties with the finances," Debbie openly explains. "It's hard for us because there is a lot of pressure on Jena and we're in a strange position because a normal parent is the one in control who has the job and brings in the money. But in this position, I'm the parent yet Jena's the one who brings in the money. It's taken us years to work it out. Jena has her own production company, Little Laine Productions, and I run it. I take a salary, but her salary is much bigger than mine and when we make decisions I have to talk to her about it. It's her money. And at the same time I ask her to be a child and to be respectful of me. It's a really weird relationship."

"The hardest thing I struggle with is trying to be a good daughter," Jena says. "It's easy to forget that I'm a daughter. I want independence."

Jena is a tiny waif, very childlike until she speaks—long articulate sentences about the movie industry, professionalism, feminism: "I find as a word feminism can be too limiting. It is my belief that everyone should be equal—men, women, Chinese, African-Americans, and so on. By its nature the word defines one movement. I want to be more inclusive." Some movie directors are unsure about how to interact with children, and she finds this disconcerting and annoying. She doesn't feel like a child; she feels like a professional. On the set of *Stepmom* Chris Columbus, the director, tried to bribe her to do another take. She told him he didn't need to bribe her. She was there to work. After that, they got along beautifully.

"Jena has never shown fear," Debbie says. "She always felt she could do anything. Everyone around her was nervous and afraid, but not Jena." This has served her well, as many of her roles have been emotionally challenging. As Bone in *Bastard Out of Carolina* she was physically abused and raped. Ellen

Foster is rendered an orphan. In *Stepmom* her mother (Susan Sarandon) is divorced by her father and then dies. And in *Book of Stars* she plays a girl with cystic fibrosis.

Jena was drawn to the roles because the scripts were good. She always reads her own scripts and decides for herself if she likes the role or not. In their small L.A. apartment, Jena would line the bathtub with pillows and blankets and read there because the bathroom was the only private place.

Debbie has never interfered with Jena's choices, not even with the Bone character. Even though Jena was only ten, she understood the script and wanted to rise to the challenge. "Everyone was worried that it would somehow hurt me. That's all the reporters asked about. But that's not me. I wasn't raped. That was Bone, her sad story."

"She's always been this way," Debbie says. "She was born this way, with an innate talent for knowing herself and knowing what's right."

"When I was little," Jena says, "I always wanted to be an actor or a singer or a teacher or a writer or a dancer. I said those are the five things I want to be and if I'm any one of them by the time I'm forty, I'll be very happy." She smiles at the irony and then takes us off to her bedroom to show us her collection of butterflies and stuffed animals. She models a Marilyn Monroe costume that she made for Halloween. In a strapless satin gown, a black and white boa around her neck, and black sunglasses studded with rhinestones, she looks direct, unsmiling, severe, wise, glamorous, a rising star, thirteen.

KATIE DAVIS, BRITTNEY GREEN,
AMANDA HERRERA, QIANA ROSADO, SHANNON
STEWART, AND CHRISA THOMAS
—
Unicyclists

The banter flies freely between Frederick Johnson, an athletic man in his midsixties, and the six ten- to twelve-year-old girls whisking around the Joan of Arc Middle School gym on their unicycles.

"If you guys don't get more serious about practicing, you'll never make it to the nationals in Seattle this year," Mr. Johnson scolds.

"Keep an open mind, Mr. Johnson."

"Believe in us, Mr. Johnson."

"Just prove me wrong," he counters, shaking his head.

Mr. Johnson, coach of the Goddard Riverside Acro Club, has been teaching unicycling to inner-city girls for eight years. His dour exterior hides nothing of the love and enthusiasm he has for his work. After an early stint as an acrobat, he got a degree in social work. He spent most of his career teaching tumbling to disadvantaged boys from Manhattan's Upper West Side, an experience he wrote about in a 1997 book entitled *The Tumbleweeds*. But when he read about studies showing that a high percentage of girls lose their self-esteem as they enter adolescence, he decided on a girls-only policy for his Acro Club.

"Boys get a lot more attention for their sports, I mean they dominate most sports, including unicycling, so you could look at the club as an attempt to balance things out," Mr. Johnson explains. "And as for self-esteem, unicycling offers constant opportunities to feel good about yourself. There are ten levels of tricks to master."

The club is free and entirely funded by the Goddard Riverside Community Center on the Upper West Side. The girls meet twice a week after school for three hours and come from all over the city. They hear about the club through word of mouth, see girls from the Acro Club performing at all-city public-school festivals, or read about it in the press. Katie Davis's father showed her an article about Mr. Johnson's Acro Club from *The New York Times* and asked Katie if it was something she might like to try. She's been riding for a year now. "I especially love it," she says, "when I'm standing with my unicycle in the park and people come up to me and say, 'Can you really ride that?' I just love it that I can do something most people can't."

The girls choreograph their own routines—with the help of Mr. Johnson—in which they do all kinds of collaborative stunts for shows. They have ridden in parades and performed at festivals, multicultural fairs, a battered-women's shelter, birthday parties, and company picnics.

Brittney Green, a tiny girl and two-year veteran of the Acro Club, demonstrates the "giraffe," a six-foot unicycle that towers above her before she mounts. Size is clearly an issue she has risen above. She does a figure eight, then does it again backward.

"Before I did this," she tells us later, "I felt all the time I can't do this and I can't do that, but now that I can do this I feel like I could do anything."

Every year Mr. Johnson takes seven or eight of the girls to the nationals. As is his wont, he's skeptical about the girls being ready to go this year. "I'm not sure they've got the discipline to put in the practice time," he says. "Riding well, like doing anything well, takes diligence and consistency."

Even as the girls whirl around the gym like hummingbirds, one has the strong sense that they are listening to Mr. Johnson's every word.

"These girls are good, really good, they can do anything they put their minds to." He hesitates, then, it seems almost for the sake of balance, he adds, "Attendance has been poor lately."

Brittney, now back on her twenty-four-inch Schwinn, whizzes by, declaring confidently to Mr. Johnson, "See you in Seeeeeeattle."

MEGAN LEVIN

—

Harpist

With the help of her parents, and with the money she made playing at parties and weddings or providing background music for commercials, Megan Levin, a fifteen-year-old harpist, bought a used Lyon & Healy Style 23 harp for $15,500. The instrument, which stands seventy-four inches high and weighs eighty-one pounds, is made of hand-selected maple and has intricate floral and swag carvings on its column, base, and feet. Meg has long honey-blond hair and a serene manner, and appears as Victorian as her harp. She began playing when she was five.

In her ten years of playing, Meg has participated in myriad master classes with world-renowned harpists and has attended a number of harp camps all over the country, including the Salzedo Harp Colony run by Alice Chalifoux in Camden, Maine. She plays with the Austin Youth Orchestra and was selected to play in a special Suzuki concert at the World Harp Congress in Tacoma, Washington.

"I have trained both on the Suzuki method and on the Salzedo method," she explains, sitting down to play for us in her father's music studio in Austin. "Very basically, Suzuki is about listening. You listen to the music and then learn to read it. Salzedo is more about technique and physical position—you have to keep your elbows out, your fingers curved and on the tips, your thumbs high, your feet flat, and your back straight. It helps the sound. I've learned the most from Carlos Salzedo. He changed everything for the harp and made it more important and more widely known. One of his most well-known pieces is called *Song in the Night,* where you get to do lots of stuff like tap on the soundboard and play with your fingernails, stuff you don't usually do."

Meg first played the harp for money when she was eight years old; she earned fifty dollars. When her teacher found out, she was very upset because the going rate for a harpist was a hundred dollars an hour and she didn't want Meg bringing down the price. So from then on Meg has played for the full rate. She plays about three gigs a month, including a lot of weddings, often together with her father on the violin or cello, her sister on the piano, and her brother doing vocals. And through connections at her father's studio, where her seventeen-year-old sister, Shay, is a sound engineer and designer, she is hired to play background music ("mostly glissandos") for radio and television commercials. But competitions are the real challenge. She has twice been a finalist in the American Harp Society's national competition, and in 1999 she won a Grammy Award for her work on a CD with the group Los Super Seven.

It's a warm Sunday in Austin. There is little traffic and the air is still. Outside, in the parking lot of the studio, Meg plays selections from Pierné's *Impromptu Caprice,* Tournier's *Jazz Band,* and Pescetti's *Sonata in C Minor*—pieces she prepared for the national competition. Although her instrument is large, we are struck by the power and breadth of its sound as it spreads over the parking lot. A few people on the way to their cars stop and listen with us as the music becomes part of the sky.

JAIMIE JONES, TRACY JONES,
AND CATALINA MAESE

———

Ballerinas

It's October, and practice for *The Nutcracker* is well under way at the San Pedro City Ballet. Dozens of girls, reflected into infinity in all the mirrors, are floating around the studio, jumping, skipping, being lifted, twirling on pointe. Two in particular, Jaimie Jones and Catalina Maese, the company's best dancers, stand out as they are lifted and spun by partners in pas de deux. In the Christmas production Jaimie will dance the part of the Dewdrop Fairy and Catalina will dance the lead as the Sugarplum Fairy.

They are bright, committed girls who don't mind the long hours required of them—getting up each morning at five, going to school all day, dancing at night. They tell us they live for dancing and dance at least twenty-six hours a week. They've been selected to go to the very competitive Joffrey summer dance camps, and Catalina has also attended an American Ballet Theater camp. They are so busy they don't have time for us until after practice at 9:00.

The studio is in a strip mall at the edge of a busy highway. Before we ask them questions, Catalina and Jaimie twirl around the parking lot together, their tutus shimmering in the strange yellow glow of the street lights. Afterward, they sit on the curb, and as they stretch their legs, we interview them. The sounds of cars and trucks, of the busy street, flood the air. Other girls rush past, collected by mothers. This is a scene that happens in malls all across America. And it is somehow magnificent, this weird juxtaposition of a parking lot on the edge of the strip with a dance form that began over five hundred years ago in Renaissance Italy, that traveled with Catherine de Medici to France when she married King Henry II, and that a century later in 1643 was the favored dance of the newly crowned five-year-old king of France, Louis XIV. Indeed he danced ballet himself in court and in 1661 created the Royal Academy of Music and Dance. It was there that the five basic positions were established and ballet developed a set technique.

"I'm determined to make a career of this," says Catalina, "and so I have no problem giving it everything I've got—all the hours." Her black hair is pulled back into a big glossy bun. She speaks with confidence as she and Jaimie rise to practice a pas de deux. Catalina already has a career in the field. For years she has been doing commercials and has worked on the animated film *Cats Don't Dance,* for which a body was animated over her movements.

"Ballet is like entering another world. It's like entering my imagination and I can leave everything else behind," Jaimie says. "I don't have worries when I'm dancing." When she was eight years old, her father abruptly left the family and her world shattered. Suddenly her mother was single and her little sister, Tracy, developed a serious eating disorder that eventually became so grave all contact with their father had to cease. Tracy was four when he left and already a dancer, but quite soon her disease threatened her ballet. Using

Catalina's arm as a bar, Jaimie lifts her right leg out straight and raises it above her head. Her two legs form almost one vertical line. "Ballet has been associated with eating disorders for a long time," Jaimie says. "We wanted Tracy to dance but had to understand how to use it positively."

Over the course of several years, Tracy battled the disorder and even required hospitalization. Indeed, now twelve, she's a tiny fragile girl with a small, timid voice that reveals her suffering. Yet she has come a long way. With the help of Cynthia Bradley, their dance instructor and the founder of the San Pedro Dance Studio, ballet became an important source of inspiration for Tracy's recovery. "Cynthia used milestones in dance as a way to motivate Tracy to gain weight, telling her she couldn't go on pointe or participate in a performance unless she gained a certain amount of weight," Jaimie tells us.

Weight is an issue Cynthia feels strongly about, and watching and helping Tracy taught her the seriousness of the illness and ways in which dance can be used to help. As a result, Cynthia does not want concerns about weight crippling any of her dancers. She realizes that the paradigm of the thin ballerina, an ideal of George Balanchine, is a dangerous one. When the death of Heidi Guenther of the Boston Ballet in 1997 made headlines, ballet schools were

forced to take the issue seriously. Many ballerinas had become obsessed with fears of losing their positions if they gained too much weight. Some schools even had weight maximums above which the ballerinas would essentially be expelled. But post-Heidi, it seems, minimum weight limits have been imposed and psychological counseling has been made available for those suffering from eating disorders.

With her girls, Cynthia never regards weight as a problem. She seems to echo the great choreographer Mark Morris, who uses dancers of all sizes and shapes to present a more human and no less graceful production. "Weight must be handled very delicately because of the severe problems we have with anorexia in this country," she says. "I don't want to contribute to that disease in any way. When dancers are serious and devoted they will tone automatically. And that's all they need, tone."

Jaimie and Tracy's father is still not a part of their lives, but Tracy is dancing again regularly and this year has three parts in *The Nutcracker*.

"Dancing taught Tracy to express herself in a way she could not verbally," Jaimie tells us. "And as a result she became determined to keep it up and gain the weight. Ballet was ours before our father left. It's hers again now. When you do something you love and give it everything, it's yours."

TIFFANY JONES

—

Rapper

I t all started out when I was eleven years old and I was reading the rap lyrics of one of my friends and I thought, I want to do that. At first everyone said you're weak, you're not even type, but in a negative way that helped. I didn't take it as a bad thing or a good thing, I took it as you need to get better, and they hear me now and they say, ooooo, you got talent, and I like that, I like that a lot, that people can tell me how much I got better at it. Rapping, hip-hop, that's what I love to do, and you know the music is in me already so I might as well bring it out.

I'm the only girl in my rap clique. We have about fifteen rappers, and we're called the Nation of Sikc, you know like crazy. We're the Nation of Sikc because we've got a sikc wit and we rap about sikc things. My homeboy, the beatmaker, chose the name. I chose my name, Ice-Sikco, because I love eating ice. My homeboy is someone I trust, someone I grew up with, someone who taught me a lot, to mike and freestyle. It's all about rhyming off the tip of your tongue.

My motto for writing rap is Keep it real. *Every time I get a beat I write it down and I keep writing until it's finished. I got a lot of flows. Sometimes you hear the flow and the beat together and sometimes you don't. Rapping, you can be an inspiration, you can have people feel what you're trying to say, you can get it out into the open in a positive way. I rap about my life, what I've been through, what I see, how I feel, what I want to become. One of my songs is about haters. I'm just trying to send out a message that there's a lot more to do in life than hating, there's a lot of stuff in this world for you to achieve, you see what I'm saying? Here's a verse from the single I got out now with my homeboy. It's called "HIV":*

> *Let me tell you 'bout this STD called the HIV*
> *You got to watch out cuz it's spreading now a lot*
> *Be careful who you choose as your partner*
> *Cuz they might take you out*
> *You don't trust nobody*
> *You got to be careful when it comes to your body*
> *You can't see the virus, all you really know*
> *Is once you're hit you gonna die slow*
> *After that your whole life is gone*
> *People start actin' funny*
> *Your whole body starts to change and you start feeling strange*
> *I'm trying to warn you now just to wear dem condoms*

MELONIE DIAZ, PATRICIA MARTE,
GANDJA MONTEIRO, YASMEEN SANTOS, HANNAH
SCHICK, AND PAOLA SOTO

—

Playwrights and performers

On a cold Sunday afternoon in November we took the subway to the Abrons Arts Center on the Lower East Side of Manhattan. Abrons is part of the Henry Street Settlement, an arts and social-services institution renowned for its innovative programs. We had first heard of the Henry Street Settlement as children from our grandmother, who as a young woman had volunteered as a nurse there. She would cross the Brooklyn Bridge three times a week, coming from her job in a Brooklyn hospital to work in a clinic that served mostly Irish, Jewish, and Italian immigrant children.

Some seventy years later, we went to the Henry Street Settlement to see a series of one-act plays put on by the Urban Youth Theater, an Abrons Arts Center program aimed at inner-city teenagers as a way of developing new voices in American theater. The series, entitled "What's So Hard About Growing Up, Girl?" dealt with themes such as street gangs, drug abuse, and being female.

The following week, before rehearsal for a rock opera based on Rudyard

Kipling's "Mowgli's Brothers" UYT was putting on in the spring, we speak to some of the group's female members. They come from all over the city and range in age from fourteen to twenty. Patricia Marte, from the Bronx, tells us that she was always embarrassed to admit to anyone that she liked to write, but since her teacher hooked her up with UYT, she says, "I'm so proud I tell everyone. The play I wrote is, you know, a girl's story, and after the performance a man came up to me and said, 'Your play really touched me. It was as if your family was my family. You should really keep writing. Nobody has moved me before quite like you did with your play.' And I was like, Oh my God, he said that about something I wrote!"

Paola Soto, also a playwright, says, "UYT has given me so much more awareness of the world, and that gives me so much more confidence. Once your ability to analyze is nurtured on one level it translates to all other areas of your life. Your range of awareness opens out."

We talk about what it's like to be female and a performer and how girls are portrayed in the media. Hannah Schick, who was recently admitted to La Guardia High School for the Performing Arts, says, "It's important to realize that a lot of people directing the shows on TV that are portraying girls are men. What men want girls to be, what men think of girls. They do things like assume since she's wearing a short skirt, she's a slut. I think it's very different when a show is directed by a woman or by a man who can see a woman's point of view."

Unlike many of the girls we interviewed for this book, the girls at UYT proudly call themselves feminists. Yasmeen Santos, a playwright and actress, gave her definition: "For me being a feminist means going out there and doing things that bring women ahead in whatever way that may be—writing, becoming a director, whatever, getting out there doing things that are positive for women."

SHANNON CURFMAN

——

Blues-rock musician

We see Shannon Curfman perform before we have the chance to meet her—in a bar called Bogart's in the back of a bowling alley in Apple Valley, Minnesota, just outside of Minneapolis. As far as we can tell, there are no apples in Apple Valley, just strip malls. The bar is packed with screaming fans and dancers on a small dance floor. No one looks underage, but even so, a bouncer in a wheelchair checks ID's. By his side, bottles of Budweiser shaped like bowling pins rest in an enormous vat of ice. The room is dark, and a fog of cigarette smoke mingles with the humidity of sweat. Shannon, up on-stage playing a red electric guitar, sings blues rock in her big, full voice, in the spotlight. She wears tight black pants, big clunky boots, and a little spaghetti-strapped T. Sunglasses hold back her long strawberry hair. At one moment midsong, she pauses, bends her head as if in prayer. The din turns to silence. Then people begin to chant: Shannon, Shannon, Shannon. There is nothing cute or baby-doll about her. She has a serious, hard-rock, don't-mess-with-me look. Already she's a legend in town. Reviewers describe her as "a real belter, with a big Janis Joplin–like delivery," "the princess of soul," "a blues sensation." She is thirteen years old.

———

Shannon sang before she could talk. She grew up with parents who loved to listen to what Shannon calls "classic" rock—Bob Dylan, the Rolling Stones, Jimi Hendrix, Neil Young. At ten she picked up an old guitar lying around her house in Fargo, North Dakota, and started strumming it. Noticing her interest, her grandmother sent her for lessons, telling her she could do anything she wanted if she put her mind to it. She wanted to be Bonnie Raitt. Six months later, she was singing and playing "funky blues rock" in Fargo coffee shops. At eleven she was playing in clubs around the state. This led to a manager; organized engagements; a CD, *Loud Guitars, Big Suspicions*; tours to fifteen states; audiences of more than nine hundred people; a fan club; radio; and recently a trip to New York for a showcase attended by major labels.

"When I was eleven I went to a bluesfest where this guy Jeff Healy was playing," she tells us at her home in suburban Minneapolis the day after her Apple Valley performance. "He's a blind guitarist who's an amazing player." She and her parents have recently moved here from Fargo so that Shannon can be closer to her manager and the local music scene. Her mother, a tall, dark woman of Chippewa descent, has devoted her life to Shannon's career. Shannon sits in her deck chair drinking soda and eating candies. "I wanted to meet him, so I went up to his bus where he was signing photographs and I introduced myself, and he asked me if I would play him a song. I sang "Malted Milk," an old blues song by Robert Johnson. After that he asked me if I wanted to jam with him in the bus, and we did that for a while—he had to unpack his equipment—and then he asked if I wanted to come along to First Avenue, a club, and play with him there. I did, and there were over three hundred people in the audience, and we got up onstage and played and played. It was so cool. I'd never played before such a big crowd. And when we were done all these people asked me if I'd play in their club. My career grew from there."

Her first band, which formed shortly after her debut, was called Monster on a Leash. "A terrible name," she says. As she became more serious and more committed, she had to find equally serious musicians. "There was a lot of evolution. In the beginning a lot of them had day jobs and this was just a hobby. So I had to let people go and audition others. It was fun and strange because I was so young, hiring these people. But now I have a great group. We've been together six months."

On average, Shannon and her band play three to five gigs a week. She is always the youngest person in the club. "I go in, do my thing, and leave. I get a lot of people asking, 'What does a white girl from Fargo know about the blues?' but then they hear me sing and everything's cool. They know I'm serious."

Hers is a business now, and with all of the performances and the merchandise that her mother sells at shows—the CD, posters, pictures, T-shirts—she brings in a serious salary. "But there are always expenses," she says. She owns the van and trailer that the group tours with, and all the equipment; recently she had a guitar custom-designed for her. "It's beautiful. Purple, but you can see the wood grain. On the neck in abalone is my name, and the guitar will light up and have an acoustic system so it can go both ways." The one thing she doesn't pay for is music lessons and voice teachers. "I do have checkups and I know not to yell, ever," she added with emphasis. "I know what to eat and drink, to stretch my voice. It's an instrument. You've got to take care of it."

Most of her days are devoted to music. She is always finding a moment to jot down an idea for a song. (Half of the songs she sings are originals.) The band practices several times a week, and she meets frequently with her manager. Even so, school comes first. For the past few years she has been home-schooled by her mother. First thing in the morning they go to work. Her favorite subjects are history and writing. "I don't care about becoming rich and famous. I just want a life that allows me plenty of time to play. Local, national, I'll take either one. I'm not picky—just let me play. It's what I love to do."

If she does have an ambition for playing in a larger forum, it's to perform at Lilith Fair with performers like Sheryl Crow, Bonnie Raitt, Liz Phair, Emmylou Harris, Natalie Merchant, Lucinda Williams. "Sarah McLachlan has opened the doors for a younger generation of women," Shannon says, "by showing everyone that we've got what it takes—the same as men. Lilith has done a lot for women in music by making it more accessible. I'd like to be part of that." In summer of 1999 Lilith Fair had its last performance. McLachlan wanted to end when the fair and female musicians were peaking. There will be other venues for Shannon.

In fact, in the year since we interviewed Shannon, her star has been ascending fast. The legendary industry mogul Clive Davis signed her to his Arista label. A producer with an ear for women's voices, he was also responsible for signing Janis Joplin, Aretha Franklin, Whitney Houston, Patti Smith, Laura Nyro, and Sarah MacLachlan. Shannon's record has now sold over 150,000 copies and her single "True Friends" has entered the Top 10 on the *Billboard* rock charts. She's been touring tirelessly, too, performing coast-to-coast with such acts as Melissa Etheridge, John Mellencamp, George Thorogood, and the Indigo Girls. Television appearances and print publicity have followed: she has been featured in *Rolling Stone* and voted one of twenty teens who could change the world by *People* magazine.

"We're on a clear, steady rise," she says. "I've only been in the business three years, and I've never run across discrimination. I know I'm young with a long way to go, but I'm certain that at least somewhat things have changed. There are so many excellent singers who are women. People want to hear them."

SAVVY

In sixth grade, I, Jenny, wore the same outfit to school every day: navy corduroy pants and a plaid flannel shirt. In math class I was getting very high marks, and I adored my math teacher, who didn't seem to notice my existence. He never called on me when I raised my hand, never commented on my test scores. One day toward the end of the year, I wore a skirt to school. For the first time all year, my math teacher called me to the front of the class. As I made my way to his desk, my heart pounding, I alternated between hope that he was going to praise my math work and fear that I had done something wrong. When I arrived at the front of the room he said, loud enough for everyone to hear, "Jenny, you're looking especially pretty today. You should wear a skirt more often." My embarrassment was accompanied by joy at having been noticed and only mild disappointment that it was not for my math skills. I waited for him to tell me his real purpose in having me come to the front of the room—to give me back homework or a test. After several excruciating minutes, he looked up and seemed surprised to see me still standing by his desk. "You may sit down now," he said.

Twenty-five years later, a study commissioned by the American Association of University Women Initiative for Educational Equity states: "A substantial body of recent research has shown that girls are systematically, if unintentionally, discouraged from a wide range of academic pursuits. Through teaching methods and tools, counseling and gender role stereotyping, gender differences that are slight at age eight or nine become barriers to entire fields of study and, later, careers by age 15."

The girls in this section have discovered in themselves an intellectual passion and, through dedication and imagination, have developed that passion—be it chess, fishing, finance, or evolutionary biology—into a skill. All of the girls are engaged in pursuits that involve some degree of science or math, areas of study that have been notoriously resistant to the participation of women.

Today successful women scientists abound, providing role models for future generations. Microbiologist Rita Colwell is the first woman director of the National Science Foundation. Her NSF grant program, called Professional Opportunities for Women in Research and Education, is aimed at pushing women into the science and engineering mainstream. Shirley Ann Jackson, who in 1973 became the first African-American woman to get a physics Ph.D. and was the first woman to head the Nuclear Regulatory Commission, is now the president of Rensselaer Polytechnic Institute, the nation's oldest university dedicated to science and engineering; 75 percent of its students are men. For the first time in NASA's forty-year history, three women (all under age forty) hold the top posts—project manager, scientist, and engineer, in a space mission. They designed, built, and launched two intricate spacecraft, called microprobes, for a mission to search for life on Mars, thereby setting planetary exploration on a bold new course. And the first woman ever to command a space shuttle, Colonel Eileen M. Collins of the U.S. Air Force, hauled the $2.7 billion Chandra X-ray Observatory into orbit, then guided the *Columbia* space shuttle back to Earth.

In response to a *New York Times* editorial lamenting the findings of a recent study showing that high school girls use computers far less than boys, one

woman wrote *The Times* with a reminder of the feminist conundrum—is everything that males do necessarily something that females should aspire to? She pointed out that the same study showed that boys are taking fewer English classes and are dropping out of school at a higher rate than girls. "Despite this," she writes, "the study's finding would seem to suggest that girls are the disadvantaged ones in our schools. But who decided that computer literacy is to be valued above the ability to read and write well?"

Sarah A. Gavit, the head engineer of the Mars microprobes, pointed out the advantages of having active women in every field when she said, "Women have really added to the workplace because we do come at things from a different angle. For the same reason that cultural diversity works, gender diversity is wonderful, too, especially when you're trying to do something creative."

At the end of sixth grade my math teacher recommended that I be jumped ahead into pre-algebra the next year. I started wearing skirts and dresses, colored tights, and ribbons in my hair. I loved going shopping with my friends and spending hours on the phone discussing the mysteries of boys. I joined the theater club and spent every afternoon after school rehearsing for the part of Abigail in *The Crucible*. I also continued to love math and do well in it.

In college I took a physics course for nonmajors, and during the first class the teacher said, "At its highest levels, physics is metaphor." What the girls we interviewed love about science and math is very similar to what we love about writing and photography—the details, the precision, the wish to get to the heart of the matter, the metaphors, the playfulness and seduction, the unanswerable questions, the answers that only ask more questions.

KHADEEJAH GRAY

—

Chess player

Seven-year-old Khadeejah Gray lives in a four-story brownstone in Harlem. Referred to by her three siblings as Queen Khadeejah, she likes to write stories about queens, draw pictures of queens, and pretend she is a queen, but most of all she likes to take out her opponent's queen on the chessboard. She plays chess and she likes to win. She likes to play with just about anyone who is good and who doesn't talk during the game.

Khadeejah is on the Hunter Elementary School Team with eleven other kids—all boys—from the first, second, and third grades. The dining room of her house is overflowing with trophies won by all the Gray children for all sorts of things from art contests to sports, but the tallest trophy (almost as tall as she is), was won by Khadeejah at the 1998 National Children's Chess Tournament in Illinois. Wearing a T-shirt that says CHESS IN EDUCATION E=MC^2, Khadeejah explains that it doesn't make any difference to her now that she is the only girl on her school team, but initially, when she was selected for the team by her coach, Sunil Weeramantry, she wouldn't have minded the company of another girl. "The boys teased me in the beginning about how I played because they didn't believe I was a good player. But I kept playing because I liked it and because I wanted to show them how good a player I am."

When Khadeejah was three and four years old she would watch her older brother and sister play chess and beg them to let her play. They told her she didn't know a thing about chess, and she said, "I do so. The queen stands next to the king." When she was five they taught her to play. Nowadays, her older siblings refuse to play her because she's too good, so Khadeejah has been teaching her five-year-old sister, Summer, the rules of chess, and Summer is already able to get to checkmate.

Khadeejah's mother, Alexis Gray, a health care consultant, was struck by the profundity of her daughter's interest in chess when Khadeejah pointed to a single pawn sitting on a chessboard and said, "That's so beautiful, that pawn is so beautiful." At first Khadeejah cried after unsuccessful tournament games. Her mother would say, "C'mon, Khadeejah, it's just a game." Khadeejah would stop crying and say with cold seriousness, "Chess is not just a game."

At the 1998 New York City Chess in Schools Junior High Tournament, Khadeejah, who was in third grade, came in first place. And she won on a blitz (the moves are timed) against the two other students who were also undefeated. Out of about fifty kids, there were only four girls. At the 1998 National Children's Chess Tournament, she placed eighth in the country in her age group and she beat the New York State champion—a fact that makes her even prouder of her trophy. At the nationals there were more than four hundred kids in her section, fewer than twenty of whom were girls. Khadeejah was the top girl in her age group nationwide. At the 1999 nationals, Khadeejah's team won second place and she was among her team's top four players.

When she's not playing with her teammates or at tournaments, Khadeejah mostly plays chess with men. She belongs to two clubs: the Marshall Club near NYU and the Manhattan Club in midtown. Even if it means losing fairly often, Khadeejah prefers to play against highly rated chess players because she feels she learns a lot more from them than from players who are nearer her own level. When the weather is good, she also plays at Washington Square Park. But she'll play wherever and whenever an opportunity presents itself. Once, after having lunch at a Burger King on the Upper West Side, she noticed a chess shark outside on the sidewalk challenging anyone to a game. She asked to play. He scoffed, but a crowd had gathered and he finally agreed to a game with the little girl. She promptly beat him. Khadeejah's reputation has grown to such a degree that at the 1999 grand opening of the Harlem Chess Center on West 119th Street she was paired with Wynton Marsalis to play against the first black grand master, Maurice Ashley, who was blindfolded. The game lasted over two hours and ended in a draw.

Khadeejah's other interests are drawing, acting, and math. She likes math, she explains, because it is related to chess. "On the chessboard there are eight squares times eight squares, which is sixty-four squares, and half of that is thirty-two squares or half the board . . . things like that." And the intense concentration she has learned from staring at the chessboard has greatly improved both her drawing and her acting (she has been in a public-services commercial on TV). When Khadeejah grows up she would like to be a grand master in chess and a pilot.

Why don't more girls play chess? Khadeejah shrugs, then says: "I think girls don't like to be beaten by boys. I don't mind being beaten by a boy. I mind being beaten."

STEPHANIE FORMAS

—

Investor

Patty Formas picks us up in front of the Westin Hotel at the Galleria Shopping Mall in North Dallas in a dark blue Mercedes S500, big as an old Cadillac, with tinted windows and a tan-and-chocolate leather interior. Patty's daughter, Stephanie, a small twelve-year-old girl with blond hair and a thick Texas accent, sits in the spacious backseat, poised and ready to talk. Patty, a single mother, wears a black Chanel suit, blond hair wrapped in a French twist, diamonds dripping by the dozen. She is all efficiency. We are to interview Stephanie as we drive downtown to Patty's brokerage firm, Southwest Securities, where she has arranged for us to photograph her daughter on the trading floor. Patty doesn't want to waste time; she's got to get Stephanie back to school.

We hop in and Patty zips off toward the Dallas skyline rising out of the flat plains of north Texas. Stephanie starts talking. She's been buying stocks on the

Internet at Nasdaq.com for the past two years. In that time she has tripled her original investment of eight thousand dollars, part of which she earned working for her mother's computer-supplies import/export business and part of which she received as a gift from her grandfather. "At first I didn't have a lot of money to play with, but I wanted to have at least a hundred shares of each stock I bought, so I looked at strong companies that were inclining over a period of time and that sold for under thirty a share."

Patty is a day trader on the side, and it was this interest of her mother's that piqued Stephanie's curiosity and inspired her to try investing in the stock market. Patty taught Stephanie how to study graphs and the business section of the newspaper, how to read annual reports. Before long Stephanie had a notebook filled with her own graphs tracking the performance of several companies. When she saw which companies were doing the best, she selected seven with which she was familiar, buying Kmart, Pepsi, 7UP, Wal-Mart, Clare, Tricon Global Restaurants, and Texas Instruments. "I'm long-terming these, which means I'll hang on to them for at least five or ten years. I'll only sell if I see horrible, drastic downward sloping."

"I want to feel financially independent by the time I'm older," she tells us. "I don't want to have to ever rely on anybody. Knowing how to earn money makes it possible. When I grow up I want to be a fashion designer. By making my money grow now and putting it aside, I'll have money to start my fashion business when I'm older, and I won't need to take such a big loan. I'll have assets. I like that freedom. Earning power feels good, makes you feel that you have more to fall back on. And if I know how to invest now, I can do something smart with the money I earn from my business. Also it gives me something to do. I have friends that just go home and watch TV and get bored. I don't get bored."

We enter downtown, driving on the street where JFK was shot, passing by the book depository and the grassy knoll. Stephanie tells us there's a museum in the book depository. Then we disappear into the canyon of new buildings that is Dallas. The only indications that this was once a cattle town are some aging grain elevators and a front-page article in the local paper describing a new law prohibiting roosters downtown. The city is famous for its extraordinary wealth and its fine shopping. Foreign tourists visiting America often make time for Dallas just for the shopping. In fact, later in the day when we ask what we should see in Dallas, Patty and Stephanie think first of the malls.

"It's a bad time to invest right now," Stephanie warns. "Since it's April, companies are announcing their quarterly earnings and the market's ricocheting in all directions but mostly inclining in an overinflated way. I'm waiting for the summer before I buy anything more. It always slumps in the summer. Right now I'm focusing on schoolwork and basketball and puppeteering for my church."

When we ask her if she ever puts her money in mutual funds, she says, "No, that's too boring. It's more fun to pick individual stocks." When we ask if she's afraid of the bear since she's only invested in a bull market, she looks confused. "The bear," her mother reminds her. We pull up in front of the Renaissance Tower and Southwest Securities. Businesspeople in smart suits rush in and out of revolving doors with an urgency and glamor that can only be about money. "Oh, yeah," Stephanie says, remembering. And then, dismissing the notion, she says, "I'm twelve years old. I've got a long horizon."

KARA-LEE ALEXANDER

—

Lobster and tuna fisher

I like to be on the water more than anything. I suppose it's because I grew up in Maine and because my father had a tuna boat for a while. When I was in fourth grade I worked on my cousin Mark's lobster boat helping bait the traps. I loved it because there was so much to do and see—seals and fish jumping and the traps were filled with all sorts of things like crabs and sea urchins and peri-winkles and mussels and clams and I was curious about all that. On the boat my job was also to put the rubber bands on the claws of the lobsters, and once one bit my finger. Hard. I shook my hand, and the lobster just fell to pieces. They're so fragile. It died.

My parents liked that I went on Cousin Mark's boat. I had always wanted to be a ballerina. I liked all the frilly stuff about it—the pink and the lace and the tutu. So when I wanted to fish and be on the water my parents encouraged it because it was different. My dad bought me rods and took me out in his boat. When I was in sixth grade, though, my friend Morgan and I wanted our own boat, and we were going to call it Just the Girls. The boys at school would tease us because we liked to fish. Then they teased me because I wore a dress to school. They'd say, "Boys don't wear dresses. You must be a tomgirl." But I wouldn't let their teasing stop me. I enjoyed fishing too much.

Now I go striper fishing with my dad, and we also go tuna fishing—two hours out to the ledges: Kettle, Sagadahoc, Jeffries, Newledge. That's where tuna hang out. I chum with Dad, that is, we throw in cut-up dead fish to attract the tuna. It's quieter than lobstering, but I love it way out there because it's really on the water. You can't see the coast, and there are whales spurting and sharks and porpoise.

I also like jigging. I jig when I'm out there while Dad's waiting for a tuna. A jig will have about twenty hooks on it, and you drop your line down two hundred feet, then jig it up and down. It's kind of wonderful because when you haul the line in, it can be heavy because on each hook there'll be a different fish. Cod, herring, hake. But not as heavy as a line with a tuna on it. They weigh up to five hundred pounds. My dad will catch one or two a week if he's lucky. Then we take them to the dock where all these Japanese men are waiting. They go around taking bites out of all the tunas, raw, and if it's good, they'll pay a lot of money for it.

I know about the water, and I like that. I can tell if a lobster is male or female. I know which fish are where. Not a lot of people know that stuff. I also don't mind getting bloody, dirty, smelly. I'll go home take a shower and put on a dress. That's all. Then I'll put on fake nails and go shopping with my girlfriends. It's soothing to shop. When I grow up I want to be a marine biologist. You know what else I used to tell the boys that teased me? I told them to get over it. I said I can do anything I want to do. I told them sometimes I'll wear a dress out fishing if I feel like it.

SOHINI RAMACHANDRAN

—

Evolutionary geneticist

When Sohini was nine years old, she decided she would spend the rest of her life tackling problems in math and science. She was having dinner with her parents, both statisticians, in Oberwolfach, a small village in Germany where every summer conferences in math and statistics are held. Sitting with Sohini and her family at dinner were two professors, one of whom was a Fields Medalist, the highest achievement for a mathematician. Both men had spent a significant part of their careers working on Fermat's last theorem. The professor sitting next to Sohini asked if she knew the Pythagorean theorem. She told him, "In a right triangle the sum of the squares of the two legs is equal to the hypotenuse squared." Then he asked her if she knew what Fermat's last theorem was, and she said no. He wrote the problem out on her cloth napkin, and she spent the rest of dinner staring at it. When the dessert tray came, she looked at him and said, "There is no answer." Everyone at the table laughed, and the professor across the table said, "Fermat thought so too, though nobody really knows." It was then that Sohini realized that there were problems in math and science that hadn't been solved yet and that she could have a hand in solving them.

In 1998 Sohini came in fourth place in the Intel Science Talent Search (formerly known as the Westinghouse Science Talent Search) for her project entitled "Homo Sapiens and *Arabidopsis Thaliana*: Mathematical and Computer Intensive Studies of Geographic Molecular Variation." By looking at the short repetitive strands of DNA called microsatellites and calculating the number of repeats between generations, Sohini made what is called a genome map to determine genetic distance between two *Arabidopsis thaliana* or mustard plants.

As we talk to Sohini, now sixteen years old, in the living room of her parents' immaculate home in a suburb of Sacramento, she tries to make her work accessible to us.

"Strands of DNA called microsatellites are short repetitive strands in which molecules repeat up to one hundred times," she explains. "The interesting thing about them is that the number of repeats doesn't change much between parent and offspring, so you can use it as a kind of tracking device. Since you are all sisters, at some point in your genome there will be a microsatellite locus and you probably all have the same number of repeats, say around twenty-five. If you have a person's whole genome map, you can compute a genetic distance."

We nod blankly and she tries again, eager to have us understand.

"The larger purpose of my work is to see how evolution occurred by looking at these plants—how our culture may have evolved. An interesting result of my project is that when I looked at the Old World and New World plants—

Krishna—the flute player

A charioteer

Saraswathi—goddess of knowledge

Shiva—lord of the dance

those plants from Europe and North Africa and those from North America—I found that they diverged genetically thirty thousand years ago, which is right when man was supposedly crossing the Bering Strait ice bridge—from the Siberian peninsula into Alaska. So maybe human intervention played a role in bringing this plant into America all the way from Europe where it genetically originated. But what really excites me is how you can use computer science and math, which are really abstract, to see how man has moved and evolved over time. In other words," she says smiling widely, "I get to use numbers to interpret nature."

Sohini has had all sorts of role models and inspirations in the many mathematicians and scientists she has met through her travels with her parents—which included a stay at the Institute for Advanced Study in Princeton—and on her own. As a reward for being the top science student in the state of California, Sohini was invited to participate in the 1998 Nobel Prize ceremonies in Stockholm. But her most formative role model has been her older sister, who came in tenth place in the Westinghouse Science Talent Search in 1991 and who is now getting her M.D. Ph.D. at the University of Pennsylvania where she studies gene expression in mice. "When I was little, my sister, who is seven years older, would ask me to help her study for tests by giving me the questions and answers to problems and I would quiz her. I was in awe because she knew so much and flattered because she wanted me to help her. Now, whenever I am able to do something as well as she has, it makes me really proud."

Sohini is putting her fifteen-thousand-dollar prize money toward her tuition to Stanford, where she will be the only undergraduate working in Professor Marc Feldman's lab, in which mathematical modeling techniques are used to study problems in evolutionary biology. She will also be one of two girls in his lab, and we ask her if she thinks this is a problem. "No, and I think the stereo-type of science being a male-dominated field is changing," she explains. "It's a stereotype that needs to be dispelled, and the fact that more girls than boys applied to the Intel Science Talent Search is a very good sign." In 1999, in the original applicant pool of sixteen hundred, 53 percent were girls and 47 per-cent boys. The first-prize winner was fourteen-year-old Natalia Toro, whose work on neutrino oscillations may have a fundamental impact on high-energy physics.

For many years Sohini has been studying the Indian classical dance known as *bharatanatya,* and has performed both in the United States and Germany. She shows us a video of her *arangetram,* or debut into the art. We ask her to dress in her dance costume, and then she takes us out to her backyard where she performs some of the traditional dance positions, all of which have a mythological significance. As she gracefully molds her body into *Saraswathi,* the goddess of knowledge, we ask her to tell us her dream for the future.

"To win the Nobel Prize," she says, shyly, proudly, her dark eyes bright with determination.

EMILY ROSA

—

Debunker of therapeutic touch

We meet eleven-year-old Emily on a rainy afternoon in Cambridge, Massachusetts. She has come east from her home in Colorado in order to give the keynote speech at the Ig Nobel Prize Ceremony held at Harvard this year and to present an Ig Nobel Prize. The Ig Nobel Prizes were first awarded in 1990 by the *Journal of Irreproducible Results* together with the MIT Museum. The prizes are presented to scientists whose achievements cannot or should not be reproduced. Emily has been asked to give the award to Dolores Krieger, a nurse and the inventor of a healing practice called therapeutic touch.

It is a couple hours before the event, and Emily is a little nervous. With all the attention she received for her science project, devised two years earlier, debunking therapeutic touch, she says she's gotten used to public scrutiny. A lanky girl with soft eyes and a quick wit, she tells us the story of how it all began. When she was nine years old, she was watching a video with her mother, a registered nurse, about therapeutic touch, a widely practiced treatment in hospitals in which a nurse will manipulate a patient's energy field through a "laying on of hands," although no actual physical contact is involved. "Some nurses claim," Emily explains, "that we have an energy field that's like this stuff hovering two to six inches around our bodies. They say that sometimes this energy field gets roughed up and that they can heal people by smoothing it back out. That's therapeutic touch." Emily's mother was very skeptical, calling the practice a "load of bunk." When Emily had a project due for the fourth-grade science fair, she decided to test the legitimacy of therapeutic touch.

She built a testing apparatus using a cardboard box, a towel, and a voice box. She asked fifteen practitioners of therapeutic touch to participate in her experiment. Before going behind a cardboard screen with two holes cut out for their hands, the practitioners were allowed to feel Emily's energy field, especially around her hands. Then they would go behind the screen, place their hands through the holes, and Emily—having decided which hand to use by the flip of a coin—would place one of her hands over one of theirs to see if they could detect her energy field. The result: they felt her energy field when her hand wasn't there 56 percent of the time. A year later a PBS show, *Scientific American Frontiers,* got wind of the experiment and asked Emily if she would redo it for television. Thirteen practitioners came to be tested by Emily's apparatus in Fort Collins, and again they did no better at feeling Emily's energy field than if they had been guessing.

Emily's mother, stepfather, and a friend helped her to write up her findings in a paper that was submitted to and published by the *Journal of the American Medical Association.* Emily was soon being written about in newspapers and magazines across the country. Renown has been a lot of fun for Emily, and good things have come of it. She has gained entry into *The Guinness Book of World Records* as the youngest author of a serious research paper published in a medical journal, and a philanthropic foundation contributed one thousand dollars toward her future education. And she was invited to give the keynote address at the 1998 Ig Nobel Prize ceremonies.

"Because of my experiment," Emily tells a rapt audience, her previous nervousness now all humor and charm, "I actually learned a lot about my own personal energy field. Therapeutic-touch nurses have said that my field is too healthy to feel, that it is too big, that it is too little, or that it is turned off because I am a skeptic. Others say it gets blown away by the air conditioning or shoots out wildly in all directions because I'm becoming a teenager. One even said my field subconsciously misleads people—not all the time, just fifty-six percent of the time."

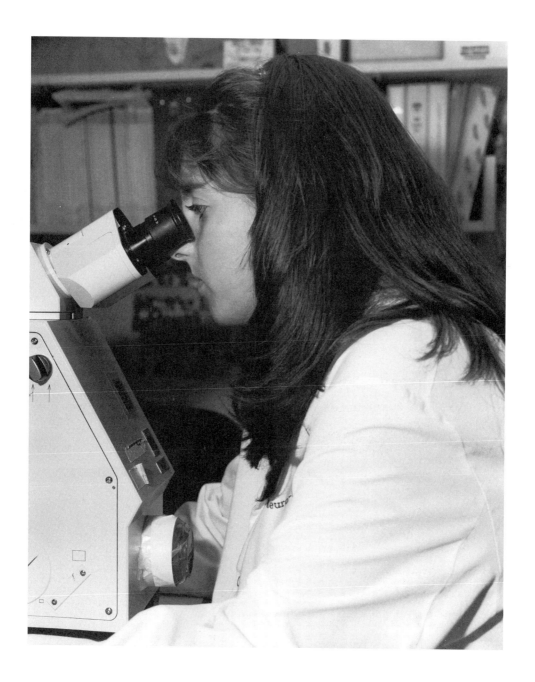

JENNIFER WILLIAMS

—

Neuro-oncology researcher

Since Jennifer Williams was fifteen, she has been organizing her life toward one goal—to become a brain surgeon. The idea was planted when she was twelve years old and watched a television documentary on the brain. "They showed surgeons removing a tumor," she explains, "and I said to myself, Oh, I wish I could do that."

Jennifer, now eighteen, grew up in Weatherford, a small town in rural Texas where she chased cows, went fishing, and hopped on and off slow trains. Despite her love for the countryside, however, she was intellectually precocious and believed that if she stayed in Weatherford, her opportunities would be limited. She wanted to make a difference in the world, and in order to do that she knew she needed a good education—something Weatherford just couldn't offer. So when she was fifteen she asked her parents—whose expectation for her was marriage after high school—if she could move to Phoenix, Arizona, to live with her aunt and be near her grandfather. "I told my mother

I wanted to go to medical school. She told me we didn't have enough money to send me to college but I was determined to prove I could succeed." They agreed to let her go.

Soon after she arrived in Phoenix, her grandfather, who works in computers, suggested she apply for a student research volunteer program sponsored by the Laboratory of Neuro-Oncology Research at Barrow Neurological Institute of St. Joseph's Hospital and Medical Center. The program selects one high school student a year for a three-year tenure requiring work at the lab three afternoons a week during the school year and for thirty to forty hours a week during the summer. Jennifer had been in Phoenix barely a month when she learned she had been accepted into the program.

When we arrive at the laboratory, Jennifer, an effervescent teenager wearing a white lab coat, is in front of a microscope examining cancerous brain cells she was growing in a flask. "It's beautiful, really beautiful," she states, urging us to have a look. In an accent that she describes as more Valley Girl than Texan, Jennifer tells us that the kaleidoscopic arrangement of dots and squiggly tadpolelike things are cells from a malignant human tumor located in the brain. "In our lab, we only deal with one type of tumor called primary tumors," she explains. "These primary tumors originate in the brain and are glioblastoma multiforms, which is a grade-four tumor and the most dangerous. It's a metastic tumor, meaning that it branches out all over your brain like veins or arteries. A person who has the kind of tumor that I am working on will probably not live more than six months after they are diagnosed."

We ask her what exactly we are looking at in the microscope. "The little balls moving around are dead cells," she tells us, "the tadpoles are cells in division, and the media I've used is fetal-calf serum because the cells grow better in it."

How can she tell something is wrong with the cells?

"The tadpoles are brain cells dividing and replicating without dying. Normal cells after a certain number of replications kill themselves in a process called apoptosis. Most of the cells you are seeing are unhealthy cells because they don't kill themselves."

——

"When I first came here," she recalls, "I was handed a stack of papers and I felt like I needed a translator to read them. I mean, I knew nothing about cancer. I knew what it was and that certain things were carcinogens, but that was it. I felt out of my league. But then I thought, if there's a will there's a way. I believe if you want something bad enough, there is a way to do it. The first six months I was here I just read."

In time, together with her program mentor, Dr. Adrienne Scheck, she developed her independent research project, which is entitled "The Role of GST Expression in the Differential Survival of Drug-Treated Cell Lines and Non-Treated Cell Lines." We ask her to describe her research in layman's terms.

"There are certain characteristics that cause cells to become cancerous in the body, and one of those characteristics is the genetics in the cells. Certain genes are turned on or off—on means working and off means not working—in the cell. There are certain genes that help a cell survive chemotherapy. Through my research I am trying to figure out how to turn off certain genes in order to increase the efficacy of chemical drugs in killing off the cancerous cells. And if I figure it out"—she laughs—"I'll have the cure to cancer."

Although Jennifer has found her work as a researcher crucial to her formation as a scientist, she has no doubt that the operating room is where she wants to be. "Everything I am doing right now is to prepare myself to be a neurosurgeon. I want to be the person who is actually in there healing the patient with the knowledge that I have." In the fall of 2000, she will begin a B.A.-M.D. program at the University of Rochester.

We ask her how she feels about the fact that her research work and the neurosurgery she aspires to inevitably involve so much contact with death.

In response, she tells a story: "This summer I was at a conference in California, and I got to see an autopsy. It was the most beautiful thing I've ever seen. I know it's, like, really morbid and everything, but we walked into the room and there was a man lying on the table and he was completely open, you could see everything, and he had died the night before, and I tried to figure out why he died. Then they sawed the skull and pulled it and then it cracked and you could see the brain and the meninges, which cover the brain. It was beautiful. I was so inspired. I mean, the brain is everything—it's what we use to see, to feel, to experience, to remember. It's life. And for me to be able to work on that, and affect that, it's just a very, very inspirational thing. While looking inside that man's brain I thought to myself, one of these days I'm going to be doing surgery. I'm going to be there."

MEREDITH CROKE

—

Climatology researcher

W hen Meredith Croke was five years old in 1985, Hurricane Gloria passed through the backyard of her Long Island home. Trees fell down, lawn furniture was overturned, and the electricity was knocked out as she, her brother and sister, and her parents sat in the living room of their house listening to the radio. Meredith isn't sure, but she believes Gloria might be the origin of her passion for weather. We meet Meredith on a sweltering, overcast midsummer day at her parents' house on Long Island Sound. The yard backs up to a sod farm. Luscious emerald grass rolls out for acres and acres beyond the row of trees at the edge of their lawn. Staring at the sea of green, one would never guess that temperatures are at a record high and rainfall at a record low, that fruits and vegetables are shriveling on the vine, and highway groundskeepers have resorted to green spray paint to hide the dried-up brown patches covering the divides.

We sit on Meredith's back porch gulping glasses of iced tea her mother made for us. Mrs. Croke tells us, "From the time Meredith was about five, we'd be driving in the car somewhere, the radio on, the kids in the back making lots of noise. But whenever the weather would come on the radio, Meredith would perk up and tell everyone to be quiet, and we'd all have to stay perfectly silent until the weather forecast was over." She tells us that when Meredith was in elementary school, she used to rush home from school to watch *Weather in the Classroom,* a program on the Weather Channel. Her friends all knew she loved the weather, so over the years she received a lot of almanacs on her birthday. When she was ten, one friend gave her a weather station, which, Mrs. Croke points out, is still attached to the porch railing. "She used to come out here every day and take notes in a little notebook describing the weather and measure rainfall," Mrs. Croke remembers. "She would cut out the weather maps in the newspaper so that she could track the weather fronts. Weather is just her thing. We have no idea where it came from."

Meredith, a very youthful nineteen-year-old with bright blond hair and round, glowing cheeks, is the principal author of a paper published in the *Journal of Climate* entitled "Regional Cloud Cover Change Associated with Global Climate Change: Case Studies for Three Regions of the United States." Her research, which she carried out under the direction of Robert D. Cess, a professor at the State University of New York at Stony Brook and an internationally renowned climatologist, will help climatologists with their models predicting what could happen with global warming. She has presented her findings to the National Weather Service at MacArthur Airport in Islip and to the Regional Weather Service at the Brookhaven Lab. When she sits down with us at the picnic table on her porch, we ask her how those presentations went.

"Really well, although I was very nervous. At Islip, as I was waiting to give

my speech, I watched about thirty professors, mostly male, sit down in the audience expecting me to tell them something new. I was pretty intimidated. But everyone was really nice and understanding and afterward I learned that almost everyone in the room was like me. They had been obsessed with the weather since they were really young."

In eleventh grade, a teacher of Meredith's who knew about her love of weather suggested she apply to the Stony Brook Young Scholars program—a summer research program for high school students. The application requires an essay describing what one wants to learn more about and why. Once accepted, the university matches the student up with a professor in the field she is interested in. "I got in and they placed me with Professor Cess," she recounts. "I later found out he wasn't too happy about it. He'd only ever worked with post-docs, not even graduate students—much less a high school student. He thought he was going to have to baby-sit me for the summer."

On her first day, Dr. Cess gave Meredith a few books and sent her down the hall to a computer and told her to familiarize herself with a certain program. "I think he was hoping he wouldn't see me again for the rest of the summer, but that afternoon I went back to him and asked him if he had something else for me to do. He was surprised that I had learned the program so quickly. He slowly kept giving me more and more things to do and I kept coming back with results—that's when he began to realize that maybe I could do something even though I was only a high school student." Meredith laughs and adds, "Now it seems Dr. Cess doesn't go anywhere without mentioning me and my work."

The project Meredith worked on that summer had to do with the relationship between global warming and precipitation in three regions in the United States. By the end of August, Dr. Cess suggested that she write up her findings and submit them for a Westinghouse Prize (now known as the Intel Science

Talent Search). She was selected as a semifinalist. The next summer she worked again in Dr. Cess's lab. He suggested she continue her research, write it up, and submit a paper to *The Journal of Climate*. She did and the paper was rejected. The journal pointed out that due to the effects of El Niño and La Niña on precipitation, her data was unreliable. The next summer, again with Dr. Cess, she switched her focus to studying cloud coverage. In December 1998, she submitted the new paper, and it was accepted in January 1999.

Soon thereafter, Meredith, who was now a student at Stony Brook, received a call from Scripps Institute for Oceanography asking her to consider going there for graduate school. And she received the invitations from the national and regional weather services to come speak about her research. "The weather world is actually a pretty small one," Meredith says.

So far, Meredith has done all her work in climatology and has yet to take any classes in meteorology. (We ask Meredith to explain the difference between meteorology and climatology: "Meteorologists predict the day-to-day weather. Climatologists look at weather trends in order to analyze what happened in the past and what might happen in the future.") Nevertheless, her plan is to become a synoptic meteorologist, the technical term for a weather forecaster. "I don't care where I do it, on TV, on the radio, at an airport, for the agriculture industry or in some marine-related field. I just want to predict the daily and weekly weather." Before that, she would like to do a stint studying extreme weather, maybe chasing tornadoes in the Midwest. "But what I love most are the more subtle changes. Just the other day, I went outside on my lunch break and it was eighty-five degrees. By the time I left for the day it was in the seventies. It was unbelievable. You expect cooling by four o'clock but not that much. It turned out a backdoor cold front had moved through. I just love that. I love the fact that the weather is always changing, and you're never really sure how it occurs or what it's going to do."

GAME

On a typical Saturday in 1973 at our house, our stepbrothers might be playing football on the front lawn. I, Jenny, would be curled up on the couch reading, Martha might be dressing her Madame Alexander dolls, and Laura was more than likely photographing the rest of us. That was the year after Title IX, the law prohibiting sex discrimination in educational programs that receive federal money, was passed. That summer, our half sister, Joan, was born, and seven years later, on a typical Saturday, our stepfather would be taking Joan to her Little League football practice (she was one of two girls on the team), or to play soccer, or later on, when she was in high school, to basketball or lacrosse.

Over the past twenty-five years the world of women's sports has experienced a revolution. Today one in three high school girls plays a sport as opposed to one in twenty-seven in 1971. Nowadays, women in sports are frequently front-page news: the women's pro basketball team the Liberty plays at Madison Square Garden, and soccer player Mia Hamm is a national hero. The 1999 Women's World Cup drew more fans (650,000) to stadiums all over the country than any other sporting event ever. Myriad studies have shown the enormous benefits experienced by girls who play sports, especially in terms of self-esteem. The athletes in this section are as diverse as the sports they play,

but the one thing they have in common with one another and with many of the girls in our book is that they love what they do and are utterly absorbed by it. Teresa Weatherspoon, point guard for the New York Liberty and devoted role model for young girls, spends a good deal of her time on and off the court inspiring girls in sports and in life. "When I'm playing and jumping and hollering, I want to pull everybody in. Feel what I feel. Feel the joy of this game— the joy of having some sort of passion for what you do. When I look up there and see those kids jumping and screaming, I know they're feeling it. That's a tremendous joy."

During the course of our research, the girls we talked to brought up the subject of Title IX again and again. Angela Ruggiero, an Olympic gold medalist in women's ice hockey, credited the statute with placing women's athletics firmly on the map in America and with significantly changing the course of her life. "The bare truth for me is that my sister never finished high school and is struggling with car payments and I'm on my way to Harvard. This is entirely due to the fact that I was able to pursue my passion and play ice hockey." The girls involved in the philanthropic group Young Women for Change were especially proud of the funding they gave to a legal aid organization specializing in bringing lawsuits against schools that were failing to comply with Title IX regulations.

Despite the huge social changes brought about by Title IX, we also heard over and over again about how boys still get preferential treatment, from better uniforms to better practice time slots, from better and more highly paid coaches to a greater variety of sports offerings. And perhaps most crippling, girls told us how school administrations, teachers, parents, and fellow students don't seem to care at all about girls' sports.

Recently, I went to a Liberty game with my three-year-old son, Tommaso,

and my sister Joan, who had played goalie for the Yale women's lacrosse team for four years. She said, "I wish I had known that I could have gone on to be a pro. It would have changed my life. If you think there is no future for your endeavors, you don't try as hard. It's easier to give up." I looked out over the stands in Madison Square Garden packed with exhilarated little girls, big girls, women, boys, and men all watching women play basketball. Teresa Weatherspoon grabbed the ball on a rebound and drove it all the way downcourt. She made one of her signature "no look" passes to Kym Hampton, another Liberty player, who successfully made an easy layup shot. Suddenly Joan, Tommaso, and I, along with everyone else in our section of the stands, leaped to our feet, raised our hands high in the air, and cheered, participating in an act of spontaneous jubilation known as a wave.

ALVINA BEGAY

—

Runner

Alvina Begay lives in Ganado, a town on a northeastern Arizona Navajo
reservation atop the Colorado Plateau. The landscape is so vast and
spare, earth and sky often seem to merge. Alvina holds the state cross-country
record for the two-mile run, which she completed in 11.16 minutes.

Before I can remember, I started running. I ran with my father. He was a na-
tional champion, a great Native American runner. My mother would try to find
me, and I'd be out with him. My father's friends would say to me, "Someday
you'll run like him," and I believed them.

The first race I entered was for a state cross-country championship when I
was in seventh grade. More than anything in the world, I wanted to win. My
father told me that if I got up before the sun and offered corn pollen to it as it

rose and if I ran east toward the rising sun and screamed as loud as I could, the holy spirits would hear me and bless me with many things. They would teach me about my strengths and weaknesses. I got up every morning and did as he said, and I won the race.

Running is in our blood; it's genetic. At races, I'll always see the Native Americans at the head. It's part of our culture, like so many things, like long hair, like my hair. My mother never wants me to cut my hair, not even to trim it, since knowledge is held in your hair. Cutting it would be like cutting off my knowledge and wisdom. It gets in the way of my speed. My trainer says I'll gain five seconds a minute if I cut it off. But I wouldn't do that, not even for running.

When Navajo girls menstruate for the first time the tradition is to have a puberty ceremony, a kinaalda. This is another tradition in which running is important to our culture. The kinaalda lasts for four days, and each morning the girls run toward the rising sun with yucca in their hair. It's a ritual reenactment of the origin myth of the Changing Woman who long ago lived all alone. One day she was lying on a rock, and she felt the presence of someone, and the someone was the sun, who impregnated her. A few days later she was impregnated again by Water Old-Man. She gave birth to twins. As they grew up, Changing Woman taught them all the things they needed to know to be good Navajos. As soon as they were old enough they left home to rid the world of evil. At the end of kinaalda the medicine men sing songs that are believed to have been first sung by Changing Woman. The songs are about beauty and power and intelligence, and they instill in the young girl Changing Woman's power.

My father taught me that I must know my culture. He said that it would help me win my races, give me that extra boost at the end, and help me cross the finish line first. After college I want to teach on the reservations. I want to teach young children what running has given me. Running is a gift in our blood that any one of us can take advantage of. My father stopped running. All his dreams vanished. I had to watch this happen. This example most of all motivates me to run and to win. I want to teach the other choices, show young Native Americans on the reservations how running has saved me.

AMANDA MIDDLETON
AND CAYLEY MIDDLETON

—

Harescramblers

Not far outside of Austin, in a field covered with Texas wildflowers—scarlet paintbrush, Mexican hats, verbena, black-eyed Susan, pink evening primrose, fleabane, bluebonnets, wild foxglove, and winecups—two sisters buzz around on their minibikes like bees drunk on honey. Amanda, who is eight and ranks seventh in the state in the 60 c.c. engine motorbike division for harescrambling, rides a green Kawasaki 60 c.c. Her four-year-old sister, Cayley, rides a yellow Yamaha 50 c.c. and wears a jersey to match and a white helmet with a pink visor and mouth guard.

Harescrambling competitions for Amanda's division usually entail a forty-five minute ride through the woods on trails that are variously covered with dirt, sand, mud, and rocks. The participants must ride around obstacles such as trees and cactus, dodge low-hanging branches, and navigate through brush.

Amanda, who loves any outdoor activity, has won a multitude of trophies for her racing and often takes them to school for show-and-tell.

Amanda is dressed in a black jumpsuit with neon green stripes, thick leather gloves, and a helmet the same color as her bike. She disappears behind a small rise in the terrain that forms a perfect natural jump. The persistent buzz of her minibike diminishes, then becomes loud as we see her fly up through the air heading in our direction. She lands, but something goes wrong and she flips over the handlebars. She hits the ground hard, her bike falling on top of her. She screams while pulling herself out from under the bike, alternately calling for her mother and crying, "My back, oh, my back hurts so much."

The color drains out of Carol Middleton's pretty round face. In a split second she is by her daughter's side calmly asking where it hurts exactly and if Amanda can move her limbs. Amanda is sobbing. Carol yells for her husband, John, who walks over to where his older daughter is lying next to her over-turned Kawasaki. He watches her for half a minute, then says gently, "You're all right, Amanda. Get back on your bike. You know you aren't ready for that jump." He resumes our conversation, answering an earlier question about the difference between motocross racing—an event in which he competes off and on—and harescrambling. "Motocross is racing around a dirt track with jumps," he explains, "while harescrambling is racing on a beaten track through the woods with various obstacles." As he talks, Amanda gets back on her bike and takes off again with an ever-so-slightly increased sense of caution.

Recent studies on women in all kinds of sports have concluded that the myth of female physical frailty has been a critical factor in hindering women's participation and success in sports. Until very recently, athletics have been typically discouraged in girls by the medical profession, which has claimed that physical exertion could endanger females' health, and especially their ability to have children. "While we've come a long way from the days when physicians warned that running could cause a woman's uterus to drop," Dr. Ellis Cashmore, author of *Making Sense of Sports,* writes, "the legacy of that kind of medical discourse is the view we still hold that women are more susceptible to damage, they are somehow more precious."

We ask John and Carol Middleton if they fear for their daughters' safety. Carol says she gets scared especially since the divisions are organized by the size of the motorbike, not by the rider's age. Since she was five years old, Amanda has competed on the track with ten- and eleven-year-old boys. (Amanda is one of two girls who harescramble competitively in her class in Texas.) But Carol says that mostly the older kids are very careful with the smaller kids and the fun they have as a family outweighs the fear. "On a motorbike girls can do anything boys can do," John adds, "which includes wiping out. It's a matter of attitude."

Amanda, sometimes joined by Cayley, who has only just begun to ride competitively, practices two to three times a week. Her goal is to ride in the Junior Supercross—a race on an indoor track replete with obstacles and jumps—held once a year in the Astrodome. She would love to buy a certain chest protector. "Not because it really protects me or anything but because it looks really cool."

TERESA GORDON-DICK

—

Greco-Roman wrestler

W restlers are a sluggish set," wrote Plato, and thirteen-year-old Teresa Gordon-Dick is inclined to agree. "I'm lazy," she tells us more than once, although we find it hard to fathom. Teresa is the national Greco-Roman wrestling champion in her bracket and the first girl to win a national wrestling title. "Three out of four pins were in under sixty seconds," she says, smiling her gorgeous smile. "My best all-time pin was six seconds." Teresa has toffee skin and ice-blue eyes, an arresting combination. She invites us into her house in rural Northern California but first shows us her animals kept in a pen: goats, chickens, ducks. Several dogs and cats roam freely. "We used to have sheep, but we ate them," she says, with a coy yet sad look—an expression she wears often. "Now we have goats and me and my brother milk them."

Teresa began wrestling by roughhousing with her brother Solomon, who, like Teresa, was adopted after spending his first years in foster homes. Teresa has five sisters and two brothers, but only she and Solomon still live at home. Teresa's father noticed her natural wrestling ability and encouraged her to compete. He acts as her trainer, sometimes paying her a dollar to run to the top of the hill behind their house. He also devises physically challenging projects like building a barn on a small piece of land they own just down the road from their house. "The only physical training I don't mind is wrestling Solomon or jumping on my trampoline," Teresa explains.

As we sit in the kitchen, Teresa tells us about wrestling. "The difference between Greco-Roman and freestyle wrestling is that in Greco-Roman a wrestler is not allowed to grab an opponent by the legs. It's all upper body." Teresa is also the 1997 novice freestyle California State champion and winner of the Western Regionals novice freestyle competition, both in coed brackets. In 1997, her banner year, she won fifty-seven matches and lost only one. Scattered throughout her house are more than forty medals and trophies she has won for her various athletic pursuits including soccer and basketball.

Teresa takes us down the road to the new barn, where her father and mother join us. The trampoline is next to the barn, and Teresa climbs on and starts jumping and doing flips. As we talk with Teresa's father, it becomes clear that his support has been crucial in a sport that is not always girl-friendly. He believes that if girls and boys were allowed to compete from a very young age, many sex roles and stereotypes would disappear. "Until girls are about twelve years old," he explains, "they are every bit as physically developed as boys and therefore should be allowed to compete in coeducational sports. When girls compete against boys, it really destroys a lot of the mythology around women being inferior physically to men. It becomes a lot harder for boys to get the idea that their sex has some sort of innate superiority which does a lot to perpetuate discrimination against women in our society."

At the National Championships there were about ten girls out of one thousand kids competing. "Teresa used to get teased a lot, and it took her a long time to build up a positive reputation as a wrestler," says her mother. "Now boys who know Teresa are proud to say they have wrestled with her, whether they won or lost." Still, Teresa adds, "It's hard on the boys to be beaten by a girl, but it's worse on the fathers. The boys get over it."

The boys Teresa competes against, however, are now entering puberty, and are fast growing bigger and stronger, making it increasingly difficult for her to wrestle with them. This is a big disappointment for her, and since there are no Greco-Roman wrestling competitions exclusively for girls (wrestling is not an Olympic sport for women), she is turning to soccer. Ranked sixth in the state for her age group, she has been chosen to be part of the Olympic developmental soccer program for girls under fourteen.

Teresa bounces high in the air, then arches her body into a backward flip— all grace and anything but sluggish.

Pole vaulter

A few years ago, when Samantha was eleven years old, she accompanied a friend to a pole-vault clinic. She excelled at soccer, basketball, and gymnastics but was looking for something different. Jeff Robbins, a track-and-field coach who was running the clinic and who is now her coach, encourages girls to try all sorts of sports that have been historically in the male domain, including pole vaulting, hurdles, shot put, and the hammer. "Traditionally, pole vaulting has been considered too dangerous a sport for women," Samantha explains. "The technique is complicated, and if the vault isn't done correctly, you can get hurt. The idea was that women would be likely not to vault correctly." We ask her if she has to be very strong to do it. "Not really," she answers. "Look at me." In her sports bra and shorts, she appears lithe and a little delicate. While strength is important, skill is far more essential to performance.

Pole vaulting is thought to have had its origin as a sport in the gymnastics events of ancient Greece, but there is no clear record of the practice. Vaulting had its more practical debut in flat marshy parts of Europe such as the fens of Cambridgeshire and Norfolk where marshes were drained by making canals. To cross these ubiquitous streams without detouring to inconvenient bridges or getting wet, people used poles, kept in stacks at each house. In the nineteenth century pole vaulting joined the roster of competitive sports, first in Germany and later at the Caledonian games in Britain. The thirteen- to fifteen-foot poles were made of hickory or some other hardwood. Samantha's pole is made of fiberglass.

Samantha, who is biracial, often travels around the country competing against female vaulters at track-and-field events. She won the Indoor National Scholastic Championships in 1997 and 1999, set meet records at the Penn Relays at the University of Pennsylvania, and won the pole-vaulting event at the National Foot Locker Championships in North Carolina. A memorable experience for her was at the Chase Millrose Games held at Madison Square Garden in 1998, the first year that women's pole vault was included. Samantha vaulted twelve feet six inches, setting a national high school record and placing fourth in the competition. In March 2000 she set another high school record, this time at the nationals in Atlanta: her vault hit thirteen feet, one quarter inch. She was chosen, along with other top high school athletes, to participate in a camp at the U.S. Olympic Training Center in San Diego and to compete in the Junior Olympics. A tenth grader, Samantha has made fast progress in pole vaulting, and now that the women's pole vault has been added to the 2000 Olympic Summer Games in Sydney, Australia, and she has qualified for the Olympic trials, Samantha has a clear objective.

LISA WELCH

—

Football player

Lisa Welch is a left tackle on the Midland Park High School varsity football team in suburban New Jersey. Across the country, just fewer than eight hundred girls have spots on boys' football teams, many as place kickers. Lisa, at five feet nine and 170 pounds, is among the first female football players in the nation to play a position on the front line.

I grew up on football, watching it on television. My mom's a big Dallas Cow-boys fan. I was a cheerleader for a couple of years, but I would watch the games instead of paying attention to the cheers. I was friends with some of the guys on the team and would tell them what they should have done in the game. They told me that if I thought I could do any better, then I should come play football myself. I took the idea up and went to the summer camp. When they saw me, they said, Oh, she's going to last a week at the most.

I've been playing since eighth grade, which was a great year, and since then I've started varsity. I got a lot of name calling from other teams, but I killed them on the field. The thing I like best about football is that I get to hit people. I've always been a very aggressive person, so going from cheerleading to football was really a relief. I started on defense. I love defense. That's where you really get to stand out. The best position I've ever played is middle linebacker. I'll admit, though, that when I go out there and see these three-hundred-fifty-pound guys, I run back to the sidelines and say I don't think I want to play today. This year is when I began to see everyone grow. Last year I was a lot bigger than some of the guys. But now I'm getting a lot smaller. Now they say I've got to gain weight, and I'm thinking I want to lose weight. I want to look like a girl, and yet if I weigh any less than I do now, I'm not going to be able to play.

My mom's got a big mouth at the games. The coach even said something to her. My dad when he heard I was playing football said, You're going to get hurt. He's never come to a game. My mom's never worried about whether or not I'll get hurt. She's worried about whether I'll make the block or tackle.

During football season I am one of the guys. I am the only player who gets cramps though. The guys on the team all know when I have my period, and they actually like it better because I'm more aggressive. The locker-room thing is a problem. They forget to open the girls' locker room for me, or sometimes they put the opposing team in the girls' locker room. Often I think girls playing is just girls trying to create their own world out of a guys' world. With guys it is natural, what they're supposed to do. Girls will always have a lot more critics. For school, I did a report on women in sports and I read an article about a coach who said a girl playing football is like taking an exam without a pencil. I'd love to meet him in person. I would go all out on him.

I can dream about playing in the NFL, but that's not reality. I mean, maybe someday as a kicker. I'd love to play for the Cowboys, but that's not reality. I can't wait to tell my children that I played football. Football is a whole different world than anything else.

—

Cheerleaders

Not far from the quiet, tree-lined neighborhood of Irving, the suburb of Dallas where Kerri, Paige, and Emily live, is the Dallas Stadium. On our way to meet them we pass the massive stadium—a ship afloat in an endless expanse of parking lot on the flat paved plains of north Texas. The Dallas Cheerleaders are, if not mythic in the American imagination, at least ubiquitous. It seems appropriate to us, then, that our cheerleaders are Texans living in the shadow of that famous stadium. Cheerleading is a big part of their lives as juniors at Irving High. They are varsity cheerleaders, they go to cheerleading camp in the summer, and they compete for and have been to the national cheerleading competition. In addition, Emily cheers for a private team, the All Star Crusaders—a Christian squad that cheers for God.

Cheerleading has changed dramatically in the past twenty years. It is now a vigorous sport that requires strength and skill and is most closely associated with gymnastics. It has also become a billion-dollar-a-year industry. There are 3.3 million cheerleaders in the nation, 95 percent of whom are female, although male participation is growing. Male cheerleaders have always taken part. Some of the more famous ones include Steve Martin, Ronald Reagan, Dwight D. Eisenhower, Senators Trent Lott and Thad Cochran, and George W. Bush.

"It used to be a girlie sport," Kerri explains, "where you just jumped up and down and wore a little skirt. Now it's starting to be a dangerous sport because the jumps are hard, you're lifting girls and throwing and catching girls, you're tumbling on grass, doing flip-flops and other stunts. Physically it's very challenging. You must be strong and very flexible. All of this requires a lot of practice, four to five times a week, and a lot of commitment. Same as with any sport. In fact, our cheerleading squad is ranked much better than our football team."

Due to Title IX, school cheerleading squads are now often required to cheer for all sports played by both girls' and boys' teams. Cheering for their football team, despite its poor season, is still the favorite of these three. "I guess I just like the tradition of it," Paige explains.

ALEXIS CHIDI

—

Figure skater

Nothing in Alexis Chidi's short history would have foretold her love for ice. The child of Nigerians who emigrated to America, she first saw figure skaters at a rink in a mall in Southern California. She was four and a half years old. Now eight, she rises at five A.M. to practice before school. Her father, a vascular surgeon, and her mother, a television actor, take turns watching her skate from the frigid bleachers at the side of the rink.

On the ice I feel like a bird, floating over it, and that's why I love to skate, that feeling. At first I was scared on the ice, and it took me a whole year to make it around the rink. But after that I started jumping, and now more than anything I like to jump, more than anything jumping makes me feel like a bird, like I'm flying. It took me three months to learn to land a triple axel, but when I did, I knew it was good, and knowing that encouraged me, made me even more committed. It makes me want to come back each day just so that I can make sure I can do it again.

My favorite part, though, is that I use my imagination, which means I'm using my brain, like with the bird and the flying. I like being out there on the ice by myself with a whole audience watching. I pretend I'm at the Olympics, or I pretend I'm a famous skater skating with grace like Nancy Kerrigan—I take ballet lessons to improve my grace—or I pretend I'm Eliza Doolittle at a tea party with friends. I invent stories to go with the music, and I play out the story on the ice in my routine—as if I were playing with dolls, telling the story to the audience. And I like that I use my brain and that skating is not just about what my body can do. Using your brain is magical.

MEGAN RANKIN

—

Barrel racer

At the edge of Vegas, to the west of town, where tract housing abruptly ends and the desert begins, the Rankins have built their new home. It's a small ranch house on half an acre with most of the yard used for their horses, roosters, chickens, dogs, and a riding ring where Megan, who is eight years old, and her brother practice their rodeo patterns at least three times a week. In front of their house the desert spreads out as far as the eye can see with the Spring Mountains rising into the bright and cloudless western sky. It is hard to believe that all the glitter of Las Vegas lies behind them, but at night an electric glow makes a dome of the sky. The sprawl of Vegas, which has been expanding at a preposterously fast rate, oozing into the desert from the center of town like a slow but steady lava flow, has enveloped them already once and forced them to move. They like to be on the edge of town so that their animals won't bother neighbors and so that they can have space for riding. Though none of them grew up on a ranch, more than anything this family likes to ride and rodeo.

When Megan was seven she had to choose between riding rodeos and appearing in beauty pageants. She'd been doing both since she was a toddler, but eventually, maintaining the two interests, with all the expenses of pretty dresses, pageant and rodeo entry fees, and a horse, was more than her family could afford. The choice, however, was easy. "I like horses much more than I like dresses," Megan said. For her mother and grandmother Megan's decision was a disappointment. "We loved dressing her up," Megan's mother said. "And going with her to the pageants. But I tell my mother that maybe someday she'll be a rodeo queen." Now Megan spends most of her free time steer daubing, pole bending, goat tying, and barrel racing. At a recent rodeo the tape of the National Anthem was forgotten, so she offered to sing it to the crowd. "I could never have done that, gotten up there in front of all those people, if I hadn't been in pageants. They gave me that kind of confidence."

At her age, boys and girls still compete against each other in the rodeo events. She can tie a goat in thirteen seconds, and in her last competition she came in third in steer daubing. She is best at barrel racing—a high-speed horseback race against time around a configuration of barrels. One of the few traditionally female events in rodeo, barrel racing originally helped the rider teach her horse to maneuver in tight spots at high speeds. Now it is a rodeo event that requires a horse bred to be fast. Megan just acquired a new horse, Naturally Up, especially for her competitions.

On weekends, with her family, Megan travels up to three hundred miles to compete in rodeos, and every Wednesday night there's a local jackpot barrel race, which she competes in for money. There's money to be made in barrel racing—anywhere from a few dollars to a few hundred. The most Megan has made at one time is sixty dollars; she uses the money to pay for her horse and its care and for rodeo entrance fees. Mostly she wins silver buckles for her belt.

Rodeos began in Texas in the 1800s as a way for ranch hands to practice roping, doctoring, and other horse-training skills. The best ranches would send their top cowboys to compete against one another as teams. In the 1920s professional rodeo was formed, and many female riders competed until Bonnie McCarroll was killed bronco riding at the 1928 Pendleton Round Up in Oregon. Following that tragedy, women were all but excluded from riding in rodeos until 1948, when seventy-four women founded the Girls Rodeo Association. Since then membership has grown to more than one hundred thousand, and riders compete at all-girl rodeos for prize money in the millions.

In her backyard ring Megan saddles Naturally Up and leads her through a few trial runs around the barrels to give us an idea of the sport. Once the horse is warmed up she trots back to starting position at the head of the ring and pauses. On the big horse Megan is tiny. Her long curly hair blows in a light breeze. Like an arrow, she darts into action and gallops to the barrels, careening around them, the horse kicking up a fine film of dust, Megan's hair flowing wildly behind her. She rides around each barrel close enough that she can touch it yet not knock it over. When she is done she repeats the configuration several more times. Her best record so far for barrel racing is 17.6 seconds. She wants to do it in 16 and says she'll practice until she does. "It's the speed I love best about barrel racing," she told us later. "The rush of it on my face and the idea that I'm making it happen."

The Spring Mountains, which look deceptively close, are actually a four-hour ride away on horseback. Megan tells us she likes to ride in the desert between her house and the foothills. She loves the quiet on the trail and, even though it appears as if nothing is out there, all the things that you can see—coyotes, rabbits, roadrunners, and quail, the elusive desert turtle, all the wildflowers in the spring. But mostly it's the riding that she loves, the feel of the horse beneath her when they're galloping out toward nowhere.

ANGELA RUGGIERO

—

Ice-hockey player

The first time Angela Ruggiero stepped onto the ice she cried. She was seven years old, and her father had signed her and her younger brother up to play with the Pasadena Maple Leaves, a junior-league hockey team at one of the few rinks near where they lived in Simi Valley, California. He dressed her in a helmet, knee pads, and shin guards, put her on the ice, and said, "Skate." She wobbled, fell, got up, fell, cried, got up, and fell again. By the end of practice that day she was cruising around the rink. Two years later she was dominating it.

"I was the only girl, and a head above all the boys," says Angela, a blonde whom it would be hard to describe as a bruiser. We are in a diner having breakfast not far from the campus of Choate-Rosemary Hall, a Connecticut boarding school where Angela is a senior. "I was an enforcer on the ice. I would go out there and kill people. Someone on the other team would call me a name, and I'd go out and get his number, take him out. I was one of the leading players."

Angela's father, a minor-league hockey player, dreamed that his son would someday play in the NHL. For Angela, his wish was that she love the sport as much as he did. "My dad had different motives for us," she explains. "He wanted my brother to go somewhere. He didn't know I *could* go anywhere, but he paid just as much attention to both of us. I sort of knew, though, that I'd never be NHL."

When Angela was fourteen, she was selected to play on the first girls' hockey team to come out of California. They went to Cromwell, Connecticut, to play against the Connecticut Polar Bears. The Connecticut coach spotted Angela and wanted her for his team. He spoke to the hockey coach and the administration at Choate-Rosemary Hall, and since Angela was getting straight As at school, admission and financial aid were arranged. Her father called her from his office a few weeks before school was to begin. "You want to go to school in Connecticut and play hockey for the Polar Bears?" he asked.

She didn't hesitate to say yes. "I had no clue I could go anywhere with this sport, that there was college hockey or the Olympics. When I went to Choate, my eyes were opened and I was inspired to achieve more. When I knew that there was something to go out there and get, that's when I really started to push myself."

At fifteen, Angela tried out for the national team and made it—as she has every year since. As the youngest team member, she was called names like Pup, but the nickname that stuck is Rugger. She began to travel, playing teams from Finland, China, Japan, and Canada. In 1998 she won an Olympic Gold Medal at Nagano. "It was literally a dream come true." She takes us to the Choate-Rosemary Hall hockey rink, where display boards are covered with ar-

ticles about her and a huge banner hangs from the ceiling congratulating her. "Competing in the Olympics," she says, "was just plain awesome. Winning was a feeling beyond words." Since the U.S. Women's Hockey Team won at Nagano, the number of female hockey players registered with USA Hockey has jumped from 5,000 in 1990 to over 25,000 in 1999. And there is serious talk of starting a women's pro league.

Angela is often asked to speak to schoolkids and community groups. "Friday night I talked to the Cub Scouts. The Cub leader told me I was the first woman they'd ever had speak to them. Whenever I talk to little boys it really strikes me because I realize that I am now a role model for them as well as for little girls."

Angela takes us to her dorm room. Naturally, it looks like a tornado hit it. The walls are covered with posters, including one of Muhammad Ali, who is her all-time hero. She grabs a Wheaties box off a shelf and shows us a picture of the U.S. Women's Hockey Team printed on the front. "That was almost as cool as winning the medal," she says. She rummages in a couple of overflowing drawers and pulls out a velvet box. In it is her Gold Medal. "Feel how heavy it is," she says, proudly handing it to us. The power of the object and of the moment brings a hush over us. "I'd like to do it again," she says softly, her bright blue eyes shimmering.

Angela, who has decided to go to Harvard, plans to be at the Olympics in 2002 and at least two more Olympics beyond that. She would love to score the winning goal in the winning game, even though she plays defense.

UNITY

The notion that community starts at home seemed to ring especially true in our family. At first there were just four of us girls in a conventional nuclear family. And then suddenly, following a series of divorces, remarriages, and a new baby, there were a total of fourteen kids in our reconfigured family, with ten of us living under one very long roof. This arrangement certainly had aspects of a community, especially as our new family often expanded to include friends, neighbors, and distant relations who either lived with us in our house or in one of the cottages and teepees dotting our wooded acres.

The lot of us were "organized" by a leader, our stepfather, and we had revolving household jobs as well as monthly "work days." The latter consisted of a full day on a weekend during which we did odd jobs, including things like painting the house, filling the potholes in the driveway, organizing the junk in the basement.

Joan, our youngest sibling and the only one related to all nine children, occupied an unusual position in the family. It was her job to be the link among us. She may have been one of ten children, but she was also the only child of her parents. From birth she had to learn diplomacy and empathy, kindness and the ability to hold herself outside the fray. Perhaps it was this role in the family that led her to be interested in larger social issues and community service. As a high school student, Joan would go regularly to a detention center in Trenton to talk with girls. In college she tutored inner-city kids in math and English. Her first job was working for the Civilian Complaint Review Board in New York City investigating police misconduct. Her next job was working for Bill Bradley's presidential campaign. Now she has decided to teach in New York City's public schools.

Our book exposed us to all sorts of girls who, like Joan, have a keen desire to participate in and contribute to the larger community. We visited local fairs and competitions such as the 4-H animal auctions at the Empire Fair and Rodeo in eastern Washington, the float-queen contests for the Battle of the Flowers Parade in San Antonio, Texas, and the Ms. Housing Authority self-esteem pageant in Newark, New Jersey. In one particularly serendipitous trip, to Grand Rapids, Michigan, we met with three different groups of girls working for social change.

We happened to hear a program on National Public Radio about a group of girls in Grand Rapids called Young Women for Change. A philanthropic organization made up of approximately twenty girls, it is given a sum of twenty thousand dollars annually by the Michigan Women's Foundation to give away to causes exclusively aiding girls and women in need. "Only three percent of all philanthropic dollars go for programs that support specifically female causes," the program's director, Kristin Gootjes, explained. "So there is still a vital need for funds that support exclusively women's issues."

On a Sunday afternoon in May in a large sunny room of a historic redbrick building in downtown Grand Rapids, where the Michigan Women's Foundation has its offices, we attend the fourth annual awards ceremony of Young Women for Change. The room buzzes with activity as the girls prepare to make speeches regarding the success of the group's year and to give out checks for several thousand dollars apiece to local organizations that help girls and young women. The 1999 recipients include Vision Quest, an alternative high school for Hispanic students that is starting a program to help girls with low self-esteem and teen pregnancy; Clinica Santa Maria, a Catholic organization addressing similar issues; West Michigan Academy of Music for Girls, which is sponsoring a choir for Hispanic elementary-school girls; and Women in the Wilderness, a six-week camping retreat for troubled girls.

As usual, choosing the grantees has been a laborious, yearlong process. The girls read numerous grant proposals and received over a hundred thousand dollars' worth of requests. They made site visits to the applicants' facilities and carefully selected the winners based on their findings. "It was gratifying to finally choose the winners," Nabiha Azam says. "When I began here, I had no idea what the word *philanthropy* meant and how much time it would take to figure out if an organization is viable and worth giving money to."

"It's a lot of hard work," Megan McElwee says. "But it puts you in touch with your community in ways that would never have occurred to me. For example, I had no idea that teenage prostitution was a problem in Grand Rapids until I started volunteering here." Some other issues that they have funded over the past four years include programs that cope with domestic violence, homelessness among youth, drug and alcohol abuse. "It doesn't matter really how much you have," Nabiha adds. "Rich or poor, just that you're willing to give—even the smallest amount of money, of time—you understand how much it can do and therefore how much you've done. It's powerful to know you have an impact." Young Women for Change has now become a national organization with offices in Denver and New York City.

———

Kristin Gootjes, the program director of Young Women for Change, put us in touch with Bettegail Shively, the director of GAP or Girls and Possibilities, another Grand Rapids group. These girls hold a yearly forum for the greater Grand Rapids public school board where seventy-five girls between the ages of ten and seventeen describe the discrimination they have experienced in their schools. We have come to talk with some of these girls at Bettegail's suburban home. The walls of her foyer are covered with handwritten lists in bold colors stating the following concerns:

- Boys don't participate as much as girls in class, yet they're automatically called on first.
- Boys and gym teachers say you throw like a girl as an insult.
- Popular girls mock unpopular girls.
- Boys mock the physical development of girls.
- Educators stereotype males and females.
- Girls put each other down.
- Girls are only supposed to play certain sports.
- After-school activities are focused on boy-oriented activities.

In the living room, girls snacking on M&Ms and nuts, soft drinks in hand, are draped over couches. In strong, vibrant voices they explain to us the nature of

GAP and the issues that have been of most importance to them this year. They are eager to share their views on eating disorders, the way women's bodies are portrayed in the media, and the pressure to be popular. The girls are most animated, however, when telling us what GAP has given them. They all want to talk at once, and even the quiet ones pipe up. "I feel we can complain without someone getting mad at us. They have to listen to us as a larger voice. And that has a more powerful impact, which they can't ignore," says Holly Morris.

"You really learn how to talk to people, to explain your concerns," Tessa Haviland adds.

"Now I think about what people say, notice it more than I had," says Meg Chamberlin. "Even when it may be unintentional, like 'You hit like a girl,' I know how to read that now, and I know how to point out to people the effect of what they're saying. People respect you more when you stand up for yourself."

Caitlin Slattery tells us that schoolmates used to tease her for dressing entirely in black. They'd ask her if she was going to blow up the school. It bothered her, of course, but eventually she learned to ask them what they meant by it and to point out to them that they were offending her because she was different. "You don't know what it means to have a voice," she says, "until you hear it speak."

As a result of the forum's efforts, girls have been heard by the local public schools and programs have been implemented to address curriculum and educator bias. And last year Bettegail received a grant of ten thousand dollars to buy books with girls and women as the main characters for the school libraries. Most of all, however, she's given these girls a clear sense of the power and importance of their own voices. She hopes that someday her program can be a model for other schools around the nation.

Bettegail Shiveley, in turn, put us in touch with Erica Curry, a veteran of the Girl Scouts and now a Teen Programs director in Grand Rapids. She runs a program within the Girl Scouts called Face-It. Teen and college-age Girl Scouts give workshops to peers and younger Girl Scouts on contemporary issues that range from the importance of reading to the consequences of smoking, from careers in math and science to suicide prevention. In a large room of the Michigan Trails Girl Scout Council headquarters in Grand Rapids, we meet some Face-It members.

"The great thing about Face-It is that it gives older and younger girls a way to get closer and help each other," says Preeya Desai. "When we talk to the younger girls, they see that when they get older they will be able to do what we're doing within the Girl Scouts."

Open to all races and religions, Girl Scouts is the largest organization for girls in the world—there are 223,129 troops in more than eighty countries—with over two and a half million members ages five through seventeen. Founded in Savannah, Georgia, in 1912 by Juliette Gordon Low, the Girl Scouts' original membership was eighteen girls including Low's niece, Daisy. Low got the idea for the organization when she met Sir Robert Baden-Powell, a British war hero, who had started the Boy Scouts in England. It was her dream to give girls opportunities to develop their potential and have fun with their peers in a supportive, all-girl setting. She did this by bringing girls out of their cloistered home environments and encouraging them to take hikes in the woods, play basketball, and go on camping trips. In 1913 the first Girl Scout handbook was published, featuring knot tying, first aid, and outdoor cooking. When Juliette Low died in 1927 the Girl Scout membership had reached 137,000, and since its founding more than 40 million women have become members.

"If you ask some random person on the street what they think of when they hear Girl Scouts, ninety-nine times out of a hundred they'll say, 'Cookies,' " says Libby Bode. "But the Girl Scouts is a lot more than that. It's about inspiring girls and building their self-respect. Face-It reinforces those goals and tells girls that they can do anything they set their minds to and deal with anything that gets in their way."

In fact, in a recent survey of more than a thousand women exploring how they became successful, Dr. Sylvia Rimm found that the Girl Scouts was extremely popular among the women in her study. In her book *See Jane Win,* Rimm writes, "Scouting became their community and an avenue for leadership, accomplishment, confidence building, and creative exploration."

Many of the girls we spoke to for this book, whether directly involved in community service or not, had given a great deal of thought to their role in the larger social fabric both as individuals and as girls. During our interview with actor Jena Malone, she told us that her favorite subject at school was English but that she was taking a really great course called Civilization. She had recently learned that the first humans were nomadic and that it was the women of these tribes who were instrumental in changing the early wandering societies into permanent communities. "Women were the first domesticators. Having planted gardens, raised animals, and given birth to children in a given place, the women found it more efficient and appealing to stay put and build on what they had begun," Jena explained to us. "I had no idea that women played such a fundamental role in our history. From the stuff you usually learn at school, sometimes you get the idea that women didn't even really exist until this century."

LIA XIONG

—

United States citizen

Lia arrived in the United States on July 24, 1986, with her five sisters, her brother, and her parents. She was three years old and a refugee from Laos, where her people, the Hmong, were being persecuted by the Communist government. Lia's family had left their mountain village in northern Laos in June of 1984. With Lia riding on her father's back, they walked for ten days without stopping to sleep until they reached the Thai border. They ate rice, used banana leaves to cover their heads when it rained, made bamboo rafts to float across the Mekong River. They were shot at by government soldiers. Once they reached the refugee camp at Chaing Kham in northern Thailand, they would wait for almost two years to get immigration clearance from the American government and for their sponsors in the United States to raise enough money for their airfare.

Sisters, cousins, nieces, and nephews pass in and out of the Xiongs' house and through the backyard where we are sitting talking with Lia. A large garden full of flowers and herbs has been planted at the far end of the yard. The fence enclosing it, made out of randomly crisscrossed sticks, has a distinctly Asian aesthetic. Lia, who plans to become a pharmacist, will later explain the medicinal purposes of some of the plants in the garden such as iris bulb for menstrual cramps and herbs for postpartum recovery.

Lia is telling us how she recently spent three weeks traveling in Laos with her parents. She is particularly proud of having made this journey using her U.S. passport. When Lia was thirteen, her greatest wish was to become an American citizen. All her friends at school were American. She wanted to travel to other countries and back to Laos. When she turned eighteen she wanted to be able to vote. She was also tired of being an alien in a country where she had lived nearly her entire life. She discovered that until she was of age, the only path to becoming an American was through her father—if he became American, she automatically would become American too. So together with two of her sisters, she began teaching her father English and helping him to study for the test the U.S. government requires all immigrants seeking citizenship to pass. In 1997 he took the test and was approved for citizenship. In 1998, after much paperwork and a swearing-in ceremony, Lia's father, Lia, and her minor siblings became U.S. citizens.

Lia's parents join us outside in the yard. They are both in their early fifties, small, the skin on their faces like soft leather. Her father is particularly handsome, his dark eyes intense and determined. Speaking through Lia—neither of them are confident using English—they tell us the story of their ten-day walk out of Laos. Lia's father decided to leave the country when the danger for his family became too great. Like thousands of Hmong men, he had worked for the CIA for ten years, from 1965 to 1975. During the Vietnam War the Hmong were recruited by the United States to fight against the Communists in what was to become known as "the secret war," since according to the 1962 Geneva Accords, U.S. military activity of any kind was not permitted in Laos. The Hmong Armie Clandestine came to number more than thirty thousand soldiers and was, at its peak, the biggest CIA operation in the world. After the Americans essentially abandoned the Hmong in 1975 (Kissinger would later lament the action in his memoirs), the Communist reprisals against the Hmong for their role in the war were extremely brutal and many Hmong were assassinated. Since then, more than three hundred thousand Hmong have fled Laos. Unlike Lia, her father and mother would love to return to their country to live, but they must wait until the political situation is more favorable. During their recent visit to Laos, Lia's father was still afraid for their safety—fighting between Hmong tribes in the north and the Communist government persists—but his desire to see his homeland outweighed his fear.

Now that Lia has her passport, her dreams of travel are far more tangible. She plans to go to Canada and to China after she graduates from high school. She wants to go to China because that is where the Hmong originally came from and where there is still a large settlement, though Chinese Hmong speak a different language from that of Laotian Hmong. "I am an American citizen," she says, her dark eyes flickering with delight, "but my spirit is Hmong."

LISA APPEL, STEPHANIE APPEL, KATIE BURNS,
CORA FISHER, KELSEY McCARTNEY, SARAH McKNIGHT,
RACHEL MOTTERAM, KIMI SLONAKER, KRIS STASKA,
AND GERALDINE STEIGER

—

Future Farmers of America at the Palouse Empire Fair and Rodeo

We drive through the tiny town of Colfax at dusk on an early September evening, headed to the Palouse Empire Fair and Rodeo, to interview a sixteen-year-old who intends to win the title of rodeo queen this year. The flat, dry, scabby lands give way to rolling hills spreading out in all directions, covered in the beige stubble of freshly cut wheat. The golden hills look like sand dunes, and we have the impression we are in the middle of an endless desert. In fact, later we would learn that in geologic terms these are loess hills, or migrating hills of silt, blown here—as sand dunes are blown around—sometime before the end of the last ice age over ten thousand years ago. The soil that makes them is some of the most fertile in the country, and as a result this area is known as the Breadbasket. Each acre can produce as much as 150 bushels of wheat, most of which is shipped off to Japan. So precious are the crops that the rains that are essential to their success are known as "million-dollar rains."

The fair is nestled in a valley encircled by the hills. The wheat glistens in the fading light. A few stars appear in the sky beside a fingernail moon. This is the quintessential county fair, with prize quilts and jams and 4-H leaders teaching young children the business of agriculture by encouraging them to raise animals for competition. Rides swirl about us. Country music plays over a loudspeaker, and everywhere we see girls—little girls, teenage girls, girls galore. Girls dressed in ball gowns, girls in overalls, girls leading their sheep, dogs, pigs, llamas, and steer to the showing grounds.

Two cousins, Stephanie and Lisa Appel, both farmers' daughters, have been raising a sheep and a steer. Lisa, whose steer is four times her size, reads the beast poetry. In addition to their animals, both girls have long lists of the entries they've made in competitions—clothes they designed and sewed, preserves, photographs. In the summers, for extra money, they drive enormous harvest trucks through the fields carrying the wheat their fathers cut with combines. This year has been an excellent one for those million-dollar rains, and the crops have done well. But the financial crisis in Japan has left the wheat unsold and in huge heaps, wasting near massive grain elevators all over the area south of Spokane known as the Palouse. Despite the hardships of farming, Stephanie and Lisa want to be on farms for the rest of their lives. "It wouldn't make sense to be anywhere else," they say almost in unison.

We meet six-year-old Cora Fisher, whose boxer, Dunbar, has won first place for obedience. We introduce ourselves to Kimi Slonaker, a little girl with a prize pig she had to put on a diet in order to prepare him for the fair. We meet a seven-year-old blonde in a party dress and patent-leather shoes, Geraldine Steiger, who holds her prize chicken. She has just won first place in a talent contest for her singing. In a pen in the shade, twelve-year-old Rachel Motteram gives lessons to Kelsey McCartney and a group of other girls on how to

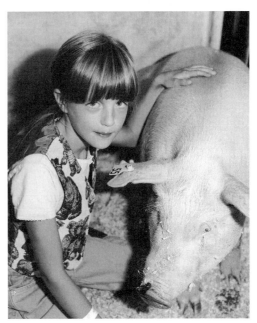

shear and card a lamb. She grooms her lamb, Dexter, while explaining to us that she's come in first in both the "meat class" and the "fitting and showing class." She has been placed seventh out of one hundred in the auction, which would give her a good shot at selling her lamb for about three dollars a pound. Her lamb weighs 150 pounds. "That's a lot of money," she says. "I'll use some of it to pay back my dad. Some of it I'll put in the bank for college, and the rest I'll keep for me." The following morning we would see Rachel, post-auction, crying, surrounded by a posse of girlfriends comforting her as she grieved for Dexter. She knew what it meant for him to be sold.

Future Farmers of America and 4-H are behind the idea of children raising farm animals. It's a way to teach the economics and realities of farming. Local businesses buy the auctioned animals—often for sums far greater than the market price—as a way to express support for the children of the community and their families.

On a lawn, a group of girls shows their llamas. Katie Burns has dressed herself and her llama in fatigues. She explains to us that her father was in the military and has just come back from nine months in Bosnia. Her favorite thing about her llama is that he gives her kisses. Kris Staska, and her llama, Hush, are dressed as peacocks, with a rainbow of feathers blossoming like a crown from their heads. "Hush got the idea to be a peacock because he lives in a corral with peacocks and he always liked the feathers. So I'm making his dream come true for one day," Kris explains. She also notes that llamas are great watchdogs; they keep the coyotes away.

As the time comes for the rodeo, we become wrapped up in the story of Sarah McKnight. For over a year she's been training for rodeo queen with the help of her best friend, Kenani LeBold, who has been serving as her trainer. Together they worked on crowd appeal, rodeo knowledge, horsemanship patterns, riding the grand entry, physical appearance, and the speech she will deliver at the judging. Preparing for the contest has cost her a few thousand dollars for clothes, makeup, saddle, and horse care, which she earned waitressing at a retirement home. Sarah is determined to win and walks around the fair with her head held high, dressed in her American stripes with her rodeo-queen contestant banner draped across her shoulder. She tips her hat, greeting people with a million-kilowatt smile—all confidence and charm, dazzling crowd appeal.

She practices her speech for us, reading it confidently; like the best politicians, she declares that she will win. Glamorous photos of her are taped to the door of her horse's stall. Inside, sequined dresses lay about on the ground, near saddles and stirrups and bags of makeup. She grabs a saddle, throws it deftly onto her horse, and buckles it up. "It's in the bag," she says. "I'll be queen." Gracefully her legs swing over the saddle and she is seated on the horse, high above us, looking down with her narrow, exacting eyes. It is easy to believe she will win.

In the event, she comes in second. "The niece of one of the judges won the title," she tells us afterward, "so I got second. I worked hard to win queen, and I know it. But there's no amount of work I could have done that would have made me better than a niece. I know that, and knowing that's enough for me."

KEEANAH BELLEMY, CONSTANCE BRANTLER, SHANIQUA BROWER, HANEEFAH CUMMINGS, MALIKAH CUMMINGS, SHAKIMAH CUMMINGS, SAKINAH DORTCH, MONIQUE DUNGEE, TAWANA ELLIS, NEVADA HALL, SHARIAH HALL, NAJAH HUGHES, YASMIYYAH JONES, DANIELLE MICKENS, KIMBERLY MILLER, LATOYA PRYOR, SHAUNETTA RANSOM, TAHEERAH SCRUGGS, SHAKEENAH TWITTY, AND MONIQUE WILLIAMS

—

Pageant participants

The Ms. Housing Authority Pageant, which takes place in Newark, New Jersey, in July, is emphatically not a beauty pageant. "It's not about beauty," explains the program director and founder, Emma Lucas. "It's a self-esteem pageant. I tell the girls that they are already beautiful, that the pageant is not about showing me how gorgeous they already are. This is about showing me that they have risen to a new level of self-esteem, that they can do it all."

Emma Lucas began the program in 1997. For years she had been listening to her husband, the former director of the Newark Housing Authority, lament the plight of inner-city girls—some as young as twelve—who were having babies "like running water" and therefore in need of bigger housing. "Having babies is all they know how to do, all they think they're good at," Emma, a tall, elegant woman, tells us. "Girls are not girls anymore. They're into sex and drinking and drugs from very young. They dress like they're eighteen when they're thirteen. I thought, somebody has to do something, and it's me." She shows us a study stating that 43 percent of girls entering Newark's school system fail to graduate from high school and that more than half of Newark's female heads of households raising children are under eighteen.

Emma decided a self-esteem program was the best way to go about getting the girls off the street, so she applied for and won funds from the Housing Authority. "I started to organize a number of different workshops for the girls but then thought there should be some sort of finale, so I got the idea of a pageant," she explains. We are sitting around a Formica-topped table in a large classroom in the basement of the Housing Authority building in downtown Newark. It is a Tuesday evening in March, and tonight's workshop is on hair care.

"There are not a lot of inner-city extracurricular activities for girls—or for boys for that matter," says Kelley Lucas, Emma's daughter and creative director of the program. "But at least boys have street sports. Girls don't even have that. I was in a couple of pageants as a teenager, and the time I spent practicing together with the other girls did wonders for my self-esteem." Kelley is in a graduate program in computer science at the New Jersey Institute of Technology. As creative director, she is involved in every aspect of the Ms. Housing Authority program, from teaching workshops to choreographing the pageant. Whatever her future career, she says, "I wouldn't give up doing this for the world."

The Ms. Housing Authority Pageant is open and free to any girl aged thirteen to sixteen who lives in low-income housing anywhere in the state. Emma recruits from housing authorities all over New Jersey and gets a pool of about one hundred applicants. Initially, she never turns anyone away. At the orientation in January she describes to the girls the seriousness of the commitment they must make in order to participate in the program. This tends to weed out about half the girls. Beginning February 1, they meet twice a week: on Tuesday nights for workshops on self-esteem, public speaking, poise, physical fitness, job interviewing, hair and nail care, self-defense, personal hygiene, cooking, writing autobiography, arts and crafts, and social skills, and on Saturdays the girls meet from ten to six for instruction in modeling and dance. "Most of the girls want to model, so I got an instructor to show them how to walk and carry themselves. I wanted to use an interest they already had to begin building their self-esteem," Emma explains. The girls are required to attend every meeting. If you miss more than three meetings, you can't come back, and if you exhibit any kind of disrespect or discipline problem, you are out. You must also be drug- and alcohol-free for the duration of the program. By March, the number of girls usually settles in at about twenty-five.

During the week, the girls often meet for activities such as trips to restaurants, museums, movies, the theater, concerts, the zoo. As part of the cooking workshop, the girls prepare formal meals and invite their mothers. They take trips to the country, canoe trips, hiking trips. The girls are also required to complete twenty hours of volunteer work in social-service jobs.

The pageant is the culmination of six months of hard work. The girls perform a chosen talent: from singing to dance to poetry recitation to original monologue. In a masked ballroom dance, they wear masks made during a workshop. Other categories are Most Congenial, Most Spirited, Most Physically Fit, Most Graceful, and Most Impressive. The twelve judges are all professional women from the community. Each year the top three winners take a trip with Emma Lucas—they have gone to Europe and to a dude ranch. The rest of the girls go to Disney World. "There are no losers," says Emma.

"We try to keep the whole thing as entertaining as possible," Kelley adds. "It's really not a competition as much as it is an opportunity to watch these girls unveil themselves to the world. They go out there, they have fun, and they show off all the stuff they learned. They're excited about it." Some of the girls crowd around the table where we sit with Emma and Kelley Lucas. We ask a few of them what they want to be when they grow up: a lawyer, basketball player, pediatrician, actor, supreme court judge, fashion designer, photographer, beautician, doctor, model, computer programmer.

We ask the girls about their experience so far in the Ms. Housing Authority program.

"With her here?" says Shakeenah Twitty, laughing and pointing at Emma. "I'm just joking. Ms. Lucas is a mother to me. And all these girls are my sisters."

"Before I came here," Tawana Ellis says, "I didn't even know what self-esteem was. Now I think I could do anything if I worked hard enough for it."

"Our mother made us come," says Shariah Hall, speaking for herself and her twin sister, Nevada, who stands next to her. "But we are so glad she did."

"I thought the whole pageant thing was stupid, a rip-off," says Najah Hughes, "but this is for us. I tell my friends about this, but a lot of them think I'm lying."

"The worst thing is getting up every Saturday morning," says Haneefah Cummings. "The best thing is the dance lessons."

"Every girl needs an advisor," Emma Lucas tells us. "Someone to walk them through and help them get out. If I have my way—and I usually do—all of these girls will go to college."

KORY ARVIZU JOHNSON

—

Environmental activist

On Valentine's Day 1988, when Kory Arvizu Johnson was eight years old, her sixteen-year-old sister Amy died of heart disease suffered since birth. The family lived in Maryvale, Arizona, a suburb of Phoenix and a community in which there was an abnormally high number of children born with birth defects and fatal diseases. A group of local women who called themselves MOM—Moms of Maryvale—came together to research the issue and learned that the well water in Maryvale was contaminated with high levels of nitrates coming from a nearby Motorola plant. Kory's mother, Teri Johnson, decided to dedicate her life to helping other children avoid the fate of her eldest daughter by working to protect the environment.

Kory too became involved when she was just nine, gathering five kids together after school at her house where she declared herself president of Children for a Safe Environment. They began by cleaning up their neighborhoods, telling their parents to turn off the water when brushing their teeth, and making contracts with their teachers not to use Styrofoam at classroom parties. Their first protest was against the state of Arizona's practice of adding high levels of fluoride to the water supply, as it is unhealthy for young bodies to absorb. They made signs on notebook paper and went down to the state capital in Phoenix and marched around.

In 1991, when Teri encouraged Bradley Angel, the founder of Greenpeace, to come to Phoenix, he and a group of Greenpeace canvassers came to stay at Kory's house and remained off and on for two years. "The canvassers rotated, but there were always at least twelve, you know, hippies living in my house, picking me up from my dance classes, making me dinner. They were my family." Kory did not meet her father, who is Mexican, until she was thirteen. Her mother, who is half white, half Sioux, brought her up alone.

"I would go to school, come home, go to a protest, make signs, or talk on the phone to other environmental groups." She also started traveling around the country speaking on behalf of children in low-income and minority communities whose well-being has been compromised by polluting industries and waste sites. "Bradley was a great motivator. He was always on fire, and if I was shy, he just urged me to speak out."

Children for a Safe Environment received a lot of attention over the years and became influential enough for authorities to arrest its members while protesting the presence of DDT at a local landfill. Environmentalists were concerned about the effect of the chemical on the community's groundwater. Kory's mother had told her stories about how, as children, she and her brother used to chase trucks carrying DDT and play in the fog left in their wake. (Kory's uncle died of stomach cancer, and Teri, who is in her early fifties, has successfully battled breast cancer and stomach cancer and was recently diag-

nosed with colon cancer.) At the protest, Teri stood in the middle of the road leading to the landfill. The approaching trucks carrying dirt contaminated with DDT did not slow down. Kory started screaming, sending the other protesters into a panic. She was arrested and taken to a holding tank in the desert from which she was released several hours later. The judge sentenced her to community service working for an environmentalist.

In 1997 Kory went to a YES camp—Youth for Environmental Sanity—run by Ocean Robbins, grandson of the founder of Baskin-Robbins. When she arrived, the other kids looked at her as if she had gotten off at the wrong stop. "I like wearing makeup and big shoes. I've never looked the part of the environmentalist—you know, khakis and Birkenstocks—it's just not me. I've always loved glitz, high heels, and long painted fingernails. My appearance has actually worked to my advantage—I so don't look the part of environmental activist that people really listen to what I have to say."

At the final YES camp assembly, Ocean Robbins announced that he had nominated Kory for a Goldman Prize, which is considered the equivalent of the Nobel Prize for environmentalists. Kory was enormously flattered, especially since one of her mentors, the environmental activist Terri Swearingen, had won the prize the year before. She went home and promptly forgot about the prize, thinking that she was too young to win such a significant award. A few months later the Goldman Prize committee called to tell her she had won. Not only was she stunned at the honor—she is the youngest person ever to win—but she nearly fainted when she heard the prize came with $100,000. "Not only did I immediately pay off all my student loans," Kory says proudly, "I also bought a house." She plans to donate the rest of the money to small grass-roots environmental causes, including Children for a Safe Environment.

IXEL CERVERA

—

Social activist

Ixel (pronounced "e-SHELL") is a Mayan name. Born in Mérida, the capital of the state of Yucatán in Mexico, she lived there until she was fourteen. When she was born, her mother, an American married to a Mexican, gave Ixel her name against her husband's wishes. He would have preferred his daughter to have a more traditionally Mexican name.

"I like being able to break barriers, to do things that I wouldn't be expected to do, and be able to prove to people that I can do whatever I want to, especially when people say to me that I can't," she tells us over breakfast in a crowded diner in lower Manhattan.

When Ixel was fourteen she decided to leave Mexico and come to New York to live with her grandmother and go to school. She had spent several summers visiting her grandparents in the city and later attending a Girl Scout camp in Vermont, which she loved. When she told her father, by then divorced from her mother, that she wanted to move to the United States, he refused to allow her to go and took away her passport. With her mother's help, she left anyway, boarding a bus for Cancún. From there she flew to Mexico City and took a bus to San Antonio. Her grandmother arranged for her to fly to New York.

Ixel, now sixteen, is thrilled to be in New York City. And from the start she has associated living there with public service, as her first school required all students to give a number of hours each year. She chose to work at NARAL, the National Abortion and Reproductive Rights Action League. She has become deeply involved with the organization, working there several hours each week. She takes her commitment to NARAL, her activism, and her feminism very seriously. "It's hard for me to see someone consider themselves a feminist and then be totally passive and not do anything about women's rights and abortion rights. You have to really do something in the community where you can say, 'I work hard for this.' *Feminist* is not just a label you can put on yourself, it's something you have to work for, just like working for a degree as an architect or a doctor. You have to earn it."

We leave the diner and walk past the Door, a youth center on Broome Street where we first met Ixel. The Door is an innovative organization that provides comprehensive services—health care, counseling, education, legal aid, arts and recreation, even an alternative high school—to people between the ages of twelve and twenty-one entirely free. Recently renovated, the stunning five-floor facility in an old warehouse boasts, among other things, an art gallery, a gymnasium, a computer center, and a youth-run café. Ixel is involved in a number of activities there. She's a member of Girlstown, a group of girls that meets once a week to talk, pamper themselves, and boost self-esteem. For a reading series called "Letters & Space" Ixel introduced Edwidge Danti-

cat, the bestselling young Haitian author. And she belongs to Be Glad, a gay, lesbian, and bisexual support group for teenagers.

We head over to the Hudson River to look for a good place to take Ixel's picture. It's a hazy day, and the Statue of Liberty is just barely visible in the distance. A Circle Line boat passes a tug pushing a huge barge loaded with cargo. We walk toward the Twin Towers, passing through a sculpture garden, and wind up at a small pond covered with lily pads. A low granite barrier surrounds the pond, and a poem entitled "The Continuous Life" by Mark Strand is engraved into the stone. Ixel reads the poem, then says, "I don't agree with what he's saying in that poem. It's much too dark."

LAUREN ALEXANDERSON

—

Starbright pioneer

In 1994, when Lauren was ten years old, she was diagnosed with osteosarcoma, or bone cancer. She had been doing tumbles in gymnastics, and her wrist began to hurt. The pain was severe enough to lead her to a doctor who found a tumor. Before long she was immersed in the harrowing world of a children's cancer ward, hooked up to IVs, undergoing numerous operations and chemotherapy, suffering from chemo fevers. For close to a year she was in and out of the hospital, her childhood emphatically interrupted or, rather, terminated. "There's no going back once you experience this. You're alone, and not even your parents can entirely understand. Though Mom and Dad had their own set of things to worry about and suffer."

Toward the end of her treatment at Mount Sinai in New York City she was asked to participate in the development of Starbright World, an interactive computer network for seriously ill children. The idea, brand-new in 1995,

promised to connect children in hospitals around the country so that they could play in a 3-D virtual playground and, for a little while, forget about their diseases. A child in New York could play with a child in Palo Alto, for example. When they tired of playing they could chat by video-conferencing. The hope was to give children back a moment of childhood so that they could regain self-esteem, talk to other kids who were suffering, and know they were not alone. Critically ill children are often forced into isolation, and Starbright intended to provide a respite from that despairing solitude.

Starbright was funded by Steven Spielberg, who soon had the support of Sprint and Intel and had recruited General Norman Schwarzkopf as a spokesman. When Lauren was first approached, she didn't know who Spielberg was, but she was eager to do something that would allow her to interact with other children. Almost immediately she met Vanessa from Palo Alto, who also suffered from osteosarcoma. They talked about everything, complained about medications and doctors and nurses. A quote that became famous at Starbright had to do with nails and hair. "Have you ever noticed," Lauren asked Vanessa, "that the chemotherapy makes your nails grow instead of your hair? I mean, really, couldn't it do the opposite?"

As one of the first children to use the Starbright system, Lauren was a pioneer and played an important role in testing programs and recommending features to serve the needs of sick children. Mostly, she told them they needed more: more programs, more games, more chat time, more computers, more access, more time. More simply because the effect was so positive. Lauren was what they called a "kid architect." In 1996 she helped launch the program in New York City, and in 1997 she traveled to the White House to show Al Gore and President Clinton how the Starbright virtual playground worked. She, along with three other kids, introduced our leaders to the various fantasy worlds that children can enter—among them a dark and cavernous cave and a tropical island paradise. In 1997 Starbright was in eleven hospitals. By 1998 it was in one hundred, all around the country. The eventual aim is to have the program available to sick kids at home.

Lauren, a blonde with a beaming smile, is now in remission. She has emerged from the cocoon of the hospital and returned to the physical challenges of life at her beloved summer house on Lake George, where swimming, diving, and sailing are her favored pursuits. However, she will always be grateful for Starbright.

The Starbright program gave Lauren a place to express both her loneliness and her creativity. Along with a group of other kids at Mount Sinai, she wrote, directed, and produced a short film explaining Starbright to other sick children. She has also participated in numerous fund-raisers. Computers are now her "practical" passion. She fell in love with them as a result of her work with Starbright and became determined to develop an alternative math class (because she hates math), her own personal website, and a website for her Lake George beach club.

"People might say, 'I know what you're going through,' but they don't have any idea what it's like to deal with bone replacement. People who haven't been there don't know what it's like to choose a cadaver bone over taking a bone from another part of your own body. Cadaver bones involve less surgery, but they don't have a reputation for lasting as long. And the idea of a dead person's bone in your body is creepy. Being able to speak with other kids who are where you are gave me more than hope, and so I'm glad I was there at the beginning of Starbright. I'm proud to have contributed my ideas."

ERICA MORAN

—

Charro Queen, Fiesta San Antonio
Battle of Flowers Parade

Every April the city of San Antonio, Texas, is inundated by Fiesta. The streets downtown are closed to cars and given to the people. Entire blocks are turned into food arcades celebrating all the different ethnicities that merge in this very vibrant city. There's a Mexican market, a German beer hall, and a taste of Cajun New Orleans. For ten days there are parades, sporting events, dances, and carnival rides. There are pageants, coronations, and queens galore: the Queen of the Order of the Alamo, the Queen of Soul, the Charro Queen, Fiesta Queen, Miss Teenage Queen, and Miss Dignity—to name only a few. San Antonian royalty roam the streets with their crowns and scepters and their thousand-dollar dresses. The banks of the slender river that snakes through the center of the town are flooded with tourists sipping margaritas, and the Alamo is alive with life. High schools and universities shut down. Businesses close their doors. Public transportation downtown is elaborately rerouted as the 3.5 million participants and spectators swarm the town to play and indulge and generate more than 220 million dollars. There is very little that a San Antonian is more proud of than Fiesta. It's a matter of civic pride; it celebrates their citizenry.

Fiesta started in 1891 when a group of women decided to honor the heroes of the Alamo and the Battle of San Jacinto by having a battle-of-flowers parade. The concept was that they would throw fresh flowers at one another in a mock battle while trotting through the streets in horse-drawn carriages. Over the years the fiesta grew up around the parade, swelling into the enormous celebration that it is today. The second-largest parade in the nation after the Rose Bowl Parade, the Battle of Flowers is still the only parade in the world run entirely by women.

We speak to one queen in particular—the Charro Queen, queen of Mexican cowboys. As Charro Queen, nineteen-year-old Erica Moran rides sidesaddle, which, she tells us, is a dying sport. Erica is one of only a few riders left in the country who has this skill. "Since women wear pants, of course, riding sidesaddle has become unnecessary, but some of us like the tradition and keep doing it." We meet her in the forming area of the Battle of Flowers Parade beneath a highway overpass. It is a hot and sultry Texas morning, and the area already pulsates with action hours prior to the step-off. Dozens of floats line the streets, and loud music seems to blast from the sky. Erica sits on her horse, Muneca, in her green *tarje*—a form-fitting long skirt and jacket. White silk flowers trim the tail and neck of her horse, and golden glitter sparkles on his hooves. Erica wears a sombrero and holds a golden whip. The wide brim of the hat shades her pretty face.

On September 11, 1998, Erica was crowned Charro Queen by the San Antonio Charro Association. Charro queens have been an integral part of the Fi-

esta for fifty-two years, and on both Sundays during the Fiesta they perform in the *charreria,* a Mexican rodeo. As the leader of the *escaramuda,* an eight-girl team of sidesaddle riders who perform tricks, the Charro Queen has a chance to show her skills. They perform eight different tricks, including a double cross, a comb, and the fan. Erica explains that to ride properly you need a special saddle that throws all your weight to the left side. In order to keep balanced you need strong thighs and excellent posture. In state, regional, and national tournaments, Erica has taken first place at one time or another.

"It takes a lot to be good at this. I got my first horse when I was seven. I did my first *escaramuda* competition when I was eleven and have been giving everything to the form since. It was for this reason that I was chosen to be Charro Queen, and I'm proud to be honoring my heritage in that way."

Before we met Erica, we wandered around the forming area guided by Teeta Ansley, a volunteer with the association that organized the parade. Though it was early, there was a biting sun. Enormous balloons shaped like cartoon animals puffed against the sky. Everywhere there were baton twirlers and tuba players and drill teams and Spanish dancers and ROTC girls and all the queens, being lifted by cranes onto their floats, standing beneath umbrellas to protect their skin from the sun. The most expensive dresses in the parade are worn by the daughters of members of the Order of the Alamo—the oldest men's group in San Antonio—and an integral part of the parade almost from its inception. These local duchesses wear heavy velvet trains embroidered with elaborate designs and fake gemstones. The trains alone cost anywhere between ten and thirty thousand dollars. The duchesses sit fanning themselves at the edges of their flowered floats waiting for the parade to step off. They are clearly the centerpiece of the parade, and as their floats roll down the main boulevard the crowd applauds them and their beautiful and intricately de-

signed gowns. On their feet they wear running shoes—a fashion touch that the crowd is aware of and begs to see as they float by. "Sneakers! Sneakers!" they cheer. And the girls lift their gowns with coy smiles.

It occurs to us that there is a hierarchy among the queens, that perhaps the Alamo girls have more status. "It's not that way," Erica explains. "We each represent our cultures. My sombrero is my crown; my golden whip is my scepter. I'm Hispanic. I always will be; my children and their children will always be too. We know our roots, the Alamo girls too. I'm keeping in touch with what it means to be Latina—though I am American and am here with wide-open arms. For example, I also dance and sing *folklorico*. San Antonio is a very mixed community. There are lots of missions here, and the flavor of the town is Mexican—Fiesta celebrates this diversity, and all of us are part of that and proud to come together in this way."

When we ask her if she considers herself more Mexican than American or more Texan than Mexican, she laughs and leans down from her horse, an entire cavalry watching behind her, and says, "I like my *munudo,* but I like my hamburgers too!"

LAURA YORKE

———

Former midshipman

*M*iss Yorke, what is that on your thumb?"

"A ring, sir."

"Miss Yorke, take it off now."

"I thought, sir, that the rules stated girls are allowed to wear one ring on each hand, sir."

"Miss Yorke, rings are allowed on your three middle fingers, not on your thumb. Take it off now."

"Yes, sir."

It was the little things. As hard as she tried, Laura Yorke could never make herself fit in at the U.S. Naval Academy in Annapolis, Maryland, where she spent the five most grueling months of her life. If she had it to do over, however, she would go through it all again, because she needed to find out if a life in the Navy was for her. If she hadn't tried it, she always would have wondered.

"Annapolis is really a great place for some people," Laura explains to us over lunch on a cold December day at her parents' New Jersey home. "What I couldn't deal with was the way they had to mold me, to break me, to make me give up who I was. My superiors always used to say, 'Miss Yorke, why are you such an individual?' and I didn't think I was acting as an individual, but there was something about me that they could tell wasn't willing to conform."

It is extremely difficult to gain admission to the U.S. Naval Academy. Not only do you need top grades and high SAT scores, but you have to pass a rigorous physical exam. You also need to procure a congressional or senatorial nomination. "I thought going to Annapolis would be like playing on a sports team, where I would be allowed to be an individual while contributing to something bigger than myself. In some senses it was like that, but they took it further. My problem was that I didn't know what I wanted to do or what I wanted to be yet, and Annapolis was not a place that would let me discover that. It was critical that I be what they wanted me to be."

From the moment she arrived on Induction Day, the first day of Plebe Summer (Plebe is the equivalent of freshman and Plebe Summer is a prolonged freshman orientation lasting three months), it became clear to Laura that there was no room for individualism and that there were no exceptions. "Everything is suddenly so abnormal. There's constant yelling, constant fear of doing something wrong. You can get in trouble so easily. Even the slightest mistake is punishable. You are training to become a machine, like when they ask you the menu for the next morning's meal." Laura begins a bullet-speed recitation: "Applejuiceorangejuicetoastmilkpancakesmaplesyrupbutter . . ." She pauses, then says incredulously, "I've already forgotten it. The point is you have to be able to react without thinking and follow orders. It's so different from the life that we have. By the end of Plebe Summer, you can't do anything for yourself, you can't even imagine being a single person. Of course, it has to be that way.

You have to be part of the whole so that in the event of a war you're not thinking, 'I'm an individual and this is my life, and I'm not sure I really want to give it up.' Rather, 'I will gladly give my life for my country, for my platoon, for freedom.' " Laura tosses her platinum-blond hair, now grown out from the required above-the-collar cut. "At Annapolis they say, 'You protect a democracy, but this isn't one.' "

Of the four thousand students at Annapolis, just under five hundred are young women. Laura tells us that she never had any problems with sexual harassment, nor did she ever feel discriminated against because she was female. "Of course, you are expected to conform, and since eighty-five percent of the students are male, that's what you conform to. There was no crying because crying is what girls do, and when I once put my hair up in pigtails in my room, a detailer screamed at me, 'What are you thinking, wearing your hair like that? Take it down.' Girls are allowed to wear earrings—only one dull gold stud in each ear—otherwise you try as hard as you can to be a boy. The girls have to constantly prove that they are equal to the boys, which means proving that they are better than equal."

In October 1997, the U.S. government dedicated the Women in Military Service for America Memorial at the entrance to Arlington National Cemetery. The memorial honors the 1.8 million women who have served in the U.S. military since the American Revolution. During the Revolutionary War, many women from the thirteen colonies joined the battle, cooking for the soldiers, sewing and laundering uniforms, and nursing the wounded. They were paid three dollars a month. Women were not allowed to enlist during the Civil War; nevertheless, some joined the fight by disguising themselves as men. More than thirty thousand women served in World War I—a third of them overseas. And during World War II more than four hundred thousand women signed up. Colonel Mary Halloran commanded the first Women's Army Corps battalion in Europe. Tens of thousands of women served in later wars—Korea, Vietnam, the Persian Gulf. The largest combat deployment of women in U.S. history took place during the Gulf War. Today there are more than three hundred thousand women in uniform.

Although American women have been serving in the military in various capacities since their country was first born, it wasn't until 1976 that the three service academies, the United States Naval Academy, the United States Air Force Academy, and the United States Military Academy, accepted their first class of women. Nowadays 80 percent of all jobs in the armed services and more than 90 percent of military career fields are open to women.

After Plebe Summer Laura was pretty miserable, but she wasn't willing to give up. Something made her want to see if the regular school year would be better. One October morning she received an e-mail from her high school English teacher. At the end was a quote from Henry David Thoreau: "Pursue some path, however narrow and crooked, in which you can walk with love and reverence. Wherever a man separates from the multitude and goes his own way, there is a fork in the road, though the travelers along the highway see only a gap in the paling."

"I realized I wasn't being true to myself," she said, clearing her throat, "that I was neither happy nor fulfilled, that I was staying at the academy because I was trying to prove something to other people and because I didn't want to let my friends down. I didn't want to be there.

"I deeply appreciated how the job I was training for was important. I felt I was doing something important every day, even as a student. You're preparing to protect your country, and that gives you a sense of pride. I wasn't particularly patriotic before I went to Annapolis, but now I have a much greater respect for the military. We put down the military a lot in this country, but there are people who work hard every day to provide the freedoms that we enjoy."

ANNE ONOUE

—

Volunteer

Anne is a leader. She's president of her senior class at the prestigious Dalton School in New York City, captain of her varsity volleyball team, secretary of a student-run charity called Common Cents, and a camp counselor for needy children in Bosnia. But she does not want to be president of the United States or any other form of politician. "What's there to believe in?" she says emphatically. "Bill Clinton? My mother's generation in the sixties had ideas, they protested, they believed. The media portrays my generation as apathetic, and it's true that many of us are. But many of us are doing good things too, and the media never bothers to spend time pointing out the good. Instead they bombard us with fear. There is so much to be afraid of—no wonder they say there's apathy."

We talk to her in her small apartment on the Upper East Side of Manhattan. Anne is an only child of a Japanese father and an American mother. Though both work in the arts, they have managed to send her to the affluent Dalton School, where some kids are dropped off in limousines and dine at Le Cirque on Saturday nights. "I don't, unless someone wants to pay for me on their credit card," Anne cracks. She's a lively girl who speaks fast and with passion and holds plenty of strong views.

"AIDS, asteroids from outer space—watch out! Armageddon!—cancer, recycling, the Ebola virus, Bosnia, Rwanda, Kosovo, Monica Lewinsky—all Monica all the time—fuel depletion, water depletion, acid rain, global warming, the end of Social Security . . . The list is endless of what our generation is being told to be afraid of, what we're being told will be used up by the time we come of age. Don't do this to us, please," she declares. "Stop throwing dead mutilated bodies at us. It's not that I don't want to know about the world. I most certainly do, but there's got to be a way to give it to us that doesn't make us shut down. I see kids critiquing life as if it were fiction."

As she speaks it is clear that she is anything but apathetic, and she credits Dalton with making her so aware. When the students begin high school they are required to do ninety hours of community service over the course of four years. "That's not a lot, but still, kids complain. I complained in the beginning, but once I took it on I realized how important it is to be involved with your community. To give to it. I tell kids now that if you don't start when you're young, you'll never do it. You won't wake up at thirty with your big job on Wall Street draining all your time and say, 'I need to do service.' "

Her first job was tutoring math students in public school, but she found the job frustrating because the kids knew nothing. "They didn't know how to add, they didn't know their multiplication tables. I'm not a math teacher. They needed so much more than I could give." In her sophomore year she became involved with Common Cents, an organization run by six students and one adult that raises money citywide by "harvesting" people's pennies. They go through entire apartment buildings door-to-door to collect unwanted pennies. They've raised over $250,000 a year. Then they encourage charities to apply for funds by submitting proposals. Based on these proposals, Common Cents decides how to distribute the money. Most of it funds community-service projects.

Twice a week Dalton has a schoolwide assembly in which current issues are discussed. Outside speakers come to talk on just about every subject—AIDS, homosexuality, fashion design. At one assembly Judith Jenya spoke about the Global Children's Organization, which she founded as a charity to support unfortunate children worldwide in an effort to give them back a tiny bit of their lost childhoods, to give them a couple of weeks to simply play. Jenya wanted volunteers to help with a camp she would be running in the summer of 1998 on a small island in war-torn Bosnia where children could act like kids. The cost was the price of an air ticket and one thousand dollars to support one child and the volunteer. "It sounded so necessary," Anne said. "When Judith described these children suffering in the midst of war, living without running water and electricity, having survived bombardments and sniper attacks and the deaths of family members, I cried. I knew I had to go." She told her parents she wanted nothing for her birthday except help toward the trip. She assisted her mother in her food-design business to earn extra cash.

In July she took a few long flights and several boat rides and ended up on the small island. In her bags she lugged teddy bears and dozens of pairs of water shoes as presents for the kids. Though there were about a hundred children in all, Anne was in charge of just two girls. "It's very one-on-one," she explains, "to give them lots of attention." The way Anne described it, the camp was run like any American summer camp, with swimming and hiking and late-night storytelling and "cool" counselors presiding over it all. "It gave me a lot to learn how to take care of these girls. When I went to Bosnia I was very much Mommy's little girl, but I changed over there. I saw what I could do for others, and that makes you grow up fast. I liked the feeling of that growth spurt. It made me realize how much I could do for myself."

The last of the afternoon sun is draining through the lacy curtains in Anne's living room, streaking her face with warm, gorgeous light. "There were also a lot of male counselors who were Bosnian, our age. I think of myself over here in America struggling with my problems, and then I think of them and it's hard to fit the two together. Ado was a guy I became good friends with. He gave me this necklace." She pulls on a simple chain around her neck to show it to us. "His uncle gave it to him and told him to give it to the first girl he fell in love with. That was me. His uncle was dying in a hospital from gunshot wounds. Ado's cousin had died a few days earlier in a terrorist massacre that Ado missed because he was fifteen minutes late to meet him. At the camp I learned how big the world is. A lot of American kids don't understand that. How good we have things—whether we dine at Le Cirque or not. My parents sleep in a Murphy bed in this room, but what does that mean? Nothing."

Again she pauses for a moment, and then she offers to show us pictures of the trip. She has dozens of snapshots—ordinary, nondescript, the campers seemingly normal little kids. "My father is Buddhist. I consider myself a Christian Buddhist. In Buddhism you believe a lot in memories. I was brought up to believe in them. That's what we have. At the end of my life I'll feel happy if I'm an old lady sitting in a rocking chair, happy with my memories. I don't need to have a billion dollars in the bank. That's also why I had to go to Bosnia, and that's why I'm going to go to Kosovo and Ireland next summer—to give those kids memories so they can pull them out of their imaginations when they need them. I suppose that's what I believe in."

AFTERWORD

Very pregnant—nine months to be exact—I, Martha, went to a political rally in New York City for the presidential candidate Bill Bradley. I stood next to a Chinese couple who, noticing my belly, gleefully told me how lucky my baby was. It's the year of the Golden Dragon, the woman said, a very auspicious year. Chinese couples have been planning babies to be born under this sign for so long that in Taiwan a 20 percent increase in births is expected this year. The sign of the Golden Dragon comes once every sixty years, and children born under it are said to be blessed with extraordinary energy and leadership skills. They are also intelligent, gifted, and perfectionists, well suited to being artists, priests, or politicians. Maybe your baby will be president, the man said, smiling a big exhilarated smile. It's a girl, I said automatically. Maybe she'll be president, he repeated just as automatically—unforced, seeming to believe just as firmly in that possibility as in the Golden Dragon. True enough, I thought. True enough for my Golden Dragon Girl.

It is 2000. The dawn of a new year, a new decade, a new century, a third millennium. Born close to the middle of the last century, my sisters and I feel privileged to occupy a position from which we can look back across the twentieth century and forward into the twenty-first, to see and imagine the world our grandmother and her mother came from and bequeathed to us and the world that our daughters and granddaughters will inherit. Our grandmother was born almost one hundred years ago on the threshold of the last century. She was the daughter of a railroad engineer and a schoolteacher living in Chillicothe, Ohio. In 1910 her mother, Glenna, did the unthinkable. Difficult and footloose, something of an adventurer, perhaps not a nurturer, she took her two young daughters and her trunk of velvet dresses and headed for Montana, leaving her husband and striking off on her own. Intrepid, our grandmother called her. She took her destiny into her own hands and lived her life as she chose, independent and self-reliant, something none of us could fail to admire. Glenna didn't imagine herself as a woman of high achievement or a woman of power. She didn't have that possibility. But the politics of this past century have changed the shape of women's lives more dramatically, more tangibly, than any other equivalent period has before. It is only now that we can, with a sense of triumph tempered by realism, have thoughts and dreams for our girls that do not exclude any career or position. Though there are still many obstacles in the path to equality, we can reasonably hope for a world where both genders will have the same choices and pursue the same passions that range from providing for children to running for president.

The girls we interviewed for this book have a very different worldview from the one we had as children. As we were growing up, girls were still taught to be nice and unchallenging, warm and gracious. Ambition was not a word in our lexicon. In elementary school, seeking biographies of important women, we found very few among the rows and rows devoted to men. Today, girls are encouraged to recognize the voices that drive them, to develop particular interests, whether genetics or music, pole vaulting or community service. And better yet, they do not have to look hard to find female role models in every field. The girls in this book taught us that they believe in themselves with a confidence that is terrifically empowering, that each of their activities gives them strength to persevere, that they are intrepid, that they are dynamic and invincible, and that the dreams they pursue have as reasonable a chance as anybody else's of coming true.

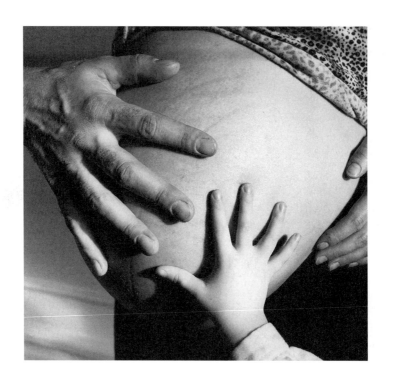

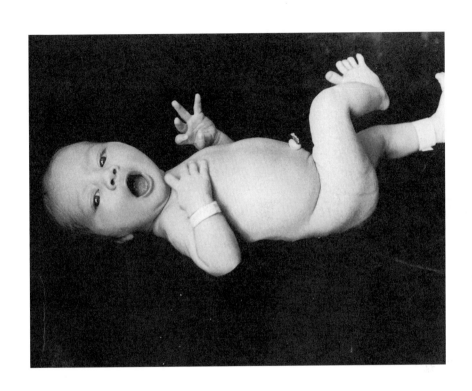

LIST OF ILLUSTRATIONS

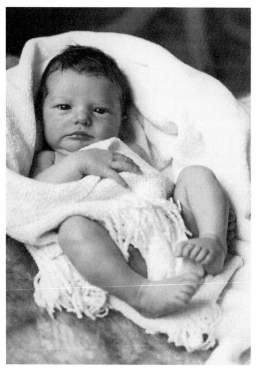

Pryde Brown

ACKNOWLEDGMENTS

First, our thanks go to all the girls whom we met and to their parents, guardians, and mentors who supported this work. We are so grateful for their openness and generosity. We'd like to thank some of the individuals who so considerately arranged meetings with girls and who gave us their time: Teeta Ansley of the Battle of the Flowers Association; Cindy Bradley of the San Pedro Dance Studio; Karen Cook of the Door; Erica Curry of the Girl Scouts; Kristin Gootjes of the Michigan Women's Foundation; Patricia Herrera of the Urban Youth Theatre; Frederick Johnson; Margie Kamine of Wings of America; Stephen Koch; Emma Lucas and Kelley Lucas of Ms. Housing Authority; Lorna Myers of the Girls Choir of Harlem; Julia Owens of America's Touch of Class; Shruthi Reddy; Jeff Robbins; Bettegail Shively of Girls and Possibilities; Dean Treadgill.

Our good friends who made substantive suggestions, offered hospitality and encouragement and sometimes their daughters, sisters, or friends include Emily Benedek; Rod and Kyle Boone; J. K. Gibson; Arielle Greenberg; Leigh Herrmann; Kira Obolensky; Larkin and Deniz Perese; Victoria Riedel; Susannah Sharpe; Cullen Stanley; Margaret Steele; and Donatella Trotti. Our thanks to all of you and to the many other friends who contributed to this book.

This book would never have been begun without the seed planted in our minds by Christopher Sweet. For that we are ever indebted. Production of this book might have faltered without the support of our agent Sarah Chalfant and her colleague Jin Auh; our wonderful editors Kate Medina and Lee Boudreaux; J. K. Lambert, our designer; and Laura's assistant, Anna Collette.

Our families, of course, deserve the last and most appreciative words: to our two other sisters Sarah and Joan, our parents, and most especially Mark, Luca, and Mark, Isobel, Tommaso, and Livia, a resounding thank you.

ABOUT THE AUTHORS

JENNY MCPHEE is a writer and translator from the Italian. She has just completed her first novel, *The Center of Things*.

LAURA MCPHEE's most recent publication (in collaboration with Virginia Beahan) is *No Ordinary Land*. She is a professor of photography at the Massachusetts College of Art and has been the recipient of a number of grants, including a John Simon Guggenheim Fellowship. Her photographs have been collected by the Metropolitan Museum of Art, the Getty Center for the Arts, and the San Francisco Museum of Modern Art, among others.

MARTHA MCPHEE is the author of the novel *Bright Angel Time* and a recipient of a National Endowment for the Arts grant for her novel in progress.